Simone de Beauvoir

Le Sang des autres

Alex Hughes

Lecturer in French
University of Birmingham

UNIVERSITY OF GLASGOW
FRENCH AND GERMAN PUBLICATIONS
1995

University of Glasgow French and German Publications

Series Editors: Mark G. Ward (German)
                   Geoff Woollen (French)

Consultant Editors: Colin Smethurst
                     Kenneth Varty

Modern Languages Building, University of Glasgow,
Glasgow G12 8QL, Scotland.

———◆———

For Martin

———◆———

First published 1995.

Printed by BPC Wheatons Ltd., Exeter.

ISBN 0 85261 462 4

Contents

Preface and Acknowledgments

In the following discussion, page references to the most recent Gallimard 'Folio' paperback edition of Le *Sang des autres* (no. 363) are given in bold type between brackets. Earlier editions are, regrettably, printed in a different typeface and with different page numbering. Quotations from other works by Beauvoir are followed by page references, in conjunction with the acronym of the title of the work from which the quotation is drawn. Details of edition and publication dates are indicated in my bibliography, section 1. Quotations taken from key works of criticism relating to Le *Sang des autres* or to Beauvoir's writing in general are normally followed in my text by the name of their author, the date of the publication if this is not self-evident, and by page references. For full details of these critical works, see the bibliography, sections 2 and 3.

A number of terms and notions drawn from Sartrean existentialism are employed in my discussion. These may not be familiar to student readers. They are marked by an asterisk, and are explained in the glossary which follows the discussion and precedes the notes. In the glossary, quotations taken from works dealing with existentialist thought are followed by their author's name, a publication date, and a page reference. For full details of these works, see bibliography, section 3.

I should like to express my heartfelt gratitude to Susan Hayward and to Ursula Tidd for the invaluable help and encouragement they offered me while I was writing this Guide.

Introduction

Beauvoir in the prewar years

For many people, Simone de Beauvoir's name is synonymous with *Le Deuxième Sexe*, her two-volume study of the feminine condition under patriarchy. Published in 1949—some twenty years before Beauvoir 'converted' to committed, public feminist activism—this work proved so ground-breaking, and so transformative of feminist thinking within and outside France, that one of the numerous obituaries which appeared in the French press in the wake of Beauvoir's death in 1986 bore the striking title 'Femmes, vous lui devez tout!' (Élisabeth Badinter, *Le Nouvel Observateur*, 18-24 avril 1986).

For other devotees of her work, Beauvoir is first and foremost an autobiographer, whose immense corpus of personal writings offers rich insights into an existence and its era. Beauvoir's designatedly autobiographical volumes are: *Mémoires d'une jeune fille rangée* (1958); *La Force de l'âge* (1960); *La Force des choses* (1963); *Une mort très douce* (1964); *Tout compte fait* (1972) and *La Cérémonie des adieux* (1981). Of these 'canonical' texts, *Une mort très douce* and *La Cérémonie des adieux* focus on (the deaths of) other people—Beauvoir's mother and Sartre—and fall perhaps less easily into the ambit of autobiography than the other works listed above, in which Beauvoir is telling her own personal story. The pendant to Beauvoir's 'official' autobiographical corpus is constituted by her *Lettres à Sartre* (2 volumes, 1990) and her *Journal de guerre* (1990). These documents were published posthumously, by Beauvoir's adopted daughter Sylvie Le Bon de Beauvoir. While they are certainly autobiographical (and highly revelatory) in their tenor, they cannot be said to belong to that body of work in and via which Beauvoir constructed her 'public' persona.

For yet other readers, the Beauvoirian text *par excellence* is *Les Mandarins* (1954), the chronicle of post-war political and sexual mores for which Beauvoir was awarded the Prix Goncourt and which she herself rated most highly amongst her novels. However, in late 1941—the point at which she began work on *Le Sang des autres*—Beauvoir had not yet produced any of her feminist or her (designatedly) autobiographical texts. Indeed, she was not yet a published writer. She was thirty-three years old, and was the author of a collection of short stories and of one novel, *L'Invitée*, which she had begun in 1938 and which was completed in the summer of 1941 (it appeared in 1943). Most unusually, for a woman of her time, she was an *agrégée de philosophie*, and belonged in consequence to France's teaching élite. She was possessed of a voracious appetite for life matched only by the voracity and intensity of her intellectual curiosity. She was the erstwhile lover—their liaison began in 1929—of Jean-Paul Sartre, the man who remained her lifelong companion and whose work is deeply imbricated with her own. She was also a woman caught up in a critical moment of history. The European crisis, the advent of war and the fall of France compelled Beauvoir to rethink many aspects of her life, including her notion of happiness, her adherence to a *modus vivendi* and a world view characterized by solipsistic individualism, and her sense of her own immunity from insecurity and accountability. The re-evaluation of self which the eruption of History into her life obliged Beauvoir to embark upon forms a significant part of the personal context within which *Le Sang des autres* came into being. Without that re-evaluation, arguably, Beauvoir's second novel could not have been written.

Le Sang des autres

Simone de Beauvoir started to work on *Le Sang des autres* during the German occupation of France. She was unable, however, to publish her novel—which may, although Beauvoir herself disliked this particular designation, on one level be classed as 'resistance fiction'—until 1945, after the Liberation. A central focus within it is the relationship between Jean Blomart, a young bourgeois who, in the course of Beauvoir's tale, foresakes the cosseted life-style of his class in order to become a printworker, a communist (briefly), a union activist, a pacifist and eventually a committed member of the Resistance, and Hélène Bertrand, the child-woman whose bond with Jean survives his 'réticences' and rebuffs, breaks down briefly after divergent attitudes to the war divide them, and is brought to an end when Hélène dies for the anti-fascist cause in which her lover—and finally she herself—come passionately to believe.

In terms of the narrative techniques Beauvoir employs in it, *Le Sang des autres* is complex, and can prove unsettling in its complexity. It is focalized through both of its principal protagonists, although Jean's voice and point of view enjoy privileged status, dominating seven of the novel's thirteen chapters. Hélène constitutes much less of a narrative force within the novel than her lover, a phenomenon underlined by the fact that in those chapters in which she is the focus of the narration (the even-numbered chapters, which, significantly, are contained and framed by/within the Blomart/odd-numbered chapters) the narrative moves predominantly into the third person, suppressing her (female) voice and restricting the reader's access to her perspective on the events of Beauvoir's tale. Temporally, the immediate narrative boundaries of *Le Sang des autres* are limited, encompassing a single night in 1942 or 1943 during which Jean, paralysed with grief and guilt as he watches beside the bed of the moribund Hélène, succeeds eventually in resolving the dilemma confronting him at the start of the novel: whether or not to sanction an act of sabotage on the part of the Resistance cell of which he is leader, an act which is in itself violent and which will provoke violent reprisals against French hostages held by the Germans.

The events of this night are generally evoked at the start and/or end of those chapters which are focalised through Blomart. However, as Jean's mind ranges restlessly over the bonds that have linked him in the past with Hélène (for whose imminent death he feels profoundly responsible), with his family, and with the cohort of friends and lovers who people the pages of *Le Sang des autres*, the work of memory and reflection considerably expands the temporal scope of the narrative, revealing to the reader the extensive prehistory of its 'present'. In this way, the details of Hélène's life and death, of the relationship she has shared with Jean over the previous decade and, most importantly of all, of Blomart's personal trajectory from boyhood onwards, are made available to us (and are dissected by Blomart).

A chronological development is respected, although the opening section of the text, marked as it is by a series of startling shifts between the variety of temporal moments covered by Beauvoir's narrative, is far from sequentially straightforward. Blomart's guilt-racked recollections and reflections attain, on occasion, a pitch of anguished intensity signalled throughout the text by the use of italics. These italicized passages focus particularly on the series of deaths that circumscribe—and embitter—Blomart's existence. They can appear radically disconnected from the main body of the narrative and, until we become used to the 'disruptions' they effect, play a not inconsiderable role in generating readerly confusion. Confusing too is the way in which Blomart, when dwelling on the self that was his in the past, employs the third as well as the first person. As Elizabeth Fallaize notes in her study *The Novels of Simone de Beauvoir*, this phenomenon may be taken, broadly, as indicative of a tendency on his part to oscillate between a retrospective perception of himself: i) as pure, autonomous subjectivity; and ii) as an 'object in the world', the product of social forces largely beyond his control, or as an *être-pour-autrui*,* a being caught and enclosed in the judgmental gaze of the Other (Fallaize, p. 47).

Thematically, *Le Sang des autres* is a rich text. As the above comments suggest (and as Chapter Two of this study will indicate further), it is in part a chronicle of desire and its discontents. It offers, moreover, insights into the political and social fabric of the turbulent era during which it is set (1930s' / 1940s' France), primarily through its account of Blomart's break with his family and milieu (chapter I) and his subsequent political development. This development highlights some of the key issues and dilemmas facing the intelligentsia of the French Left in the decade preceding the Second World War. It takes place against a backdrop detailing the 'champ politique bipolarisée' that was France in the latter part of the interwar epoch (an epoch when 'l'anticommunisme et l'antifascisme deviennent des paramètres d'engagement essentiels'[1]) the proliferation of Fascism in Europe, and the peripeteia of the French syndicalist movement and of the Popular Front (a left-wing alliance of socialists, communists and radicals which

---

[1] Pascal Ory, Jean-François Sirinelli, *Les Intellectuels en France, de l'affaire Dreyfus à nos jours* (Paris: Colin, 1986), p. 92.

came to power after the elections of 1936 with Léon Blum at its head, enjoyed mixed fortunes, and fell finally in 1938). Factors and episodes circumscribing the political context in which Blomart (together with his generation) evolves include the outbreak of the Spanish Civil War (1936-1939), the annexation of Austria by Germany and the Munich Crisis (1938), the declaration of hostilities against Germany by Britain and France (September 1939), and finally the defeat of France (June 1940) and its aftermath. All of these events are evoked or alluded to in Beauvoir's text.

The kaleidoscopic picture of the life and concerns of the people of France prior to and during World War Two presented to the reader of *Le Sang des autres* is further enhanced by the descriptions we are given of Blomart's arguments about pacifism/interventionism with Jewish political activists exiled from Austria (chapter V), of his mobilisation and his stint in the army during the 'drôle de guerre' (chapters VIII and IX), of his later activities in the Resistance (chapters VII, IX, XI, XII), of Hélène's experience of the exodus from Paris that followed the arrival of the German army in France (chapter X), and of her adventures as a civilian during the Occupation (chapters X and XII). Clearly, then, *Le Sang des autres* constitutes a tale of its time as well as a love story. It is also, though, and crucially, a text with a philosophical and moral message to impart.

Chapter One

Guilt, responsibility, freedom: the ethical bond with the Other

'Ma chute originelle, c'est l'existence de l'autre'

(SARTRE, L'Être et le néant, p. 321)

One of the key elements that characterizes Beauvoir's second novel and distinguishes it from L'Invitée is its characters' awareness of 'the fact of the insertion of their personal lives in their own time, their own period of history' (Fallaize, p. 44). The protagonists of Le Sang des autres come to confront the 'fundamental interrelation of the personal and the political', and to accept that they cannot live in isolation from the world and its events (ibid., p. 45). Beauvoir's decision to offer in her novel an account of an 'encounter with history' reflected her own experience of precisely such an encounter: an experience which coincided with the gestation of her text and which the chaos of war forced upon her. However, her selection of a moment of historico-political crisis as the backdrop for her second novel derives also—and more importantly—from the fact that a context of this kind provided her with an ideal 'stimulus to, and framework or base for, reflection on moral issues' (Keefe, 1986, p. 88).

Beauvoir's documentation of a particular—and particularly cataclysmic—slice of French history is not, then, an end in itself. The historical is inextricably linked in Le Sang des autres to the ethical; indeed, as Beauvoir suggests in her second autobiographical volume, La Force de l'âge (1960), the historical, social and political aspect of her text is effectively subordinate to 'le thème profond du livre', which is a moral and metaphysical theme: that of the human individual's 'rapport à autrui dans toute sa complexité' (FA, p. 269). A focus on the self / other relation is in fact a recurring feature of Beauvoir's œuvre and a feature present from the outset (a phenomenon which leads Margaret Simons to argue that Beauvoir's writings on alterity may have *influenced* Sartre's existentialist analyses of the problem of the Other, analyses from which Beauvoir's work is often perceived to *derive*).[1] Ultimately, this focus led Beauvoir to evolve, most notably in *Le Deuxième Sexe*, her notion of the Social Other, and to produce around that notion 'an intellectually convincing analysis of social oppression whose origins were not primarily economic' (Fullbrook and Fullbrook, p. 172). One of the early works in which she explores 'notre juste rapport avec autrui' (*FA*, p. 700) in detail, and in non-fictional form, is her philosophical essay *Pyrrhus et Cinéas*.

Pyrrhus et Cinéas, published in 1944, belongs, like *Le Sang des autres* (completed in early 1943), to what Beauvoir describes rather dismissively as 'la «période morale» de ma vie littéraire' (*FA*, p. 630), and is in some measure a sister text to her second novel. It represents an attempt by Beauvoir to explore further and otherwise 'des questions [...] abordées dans *Le Sang des autres*' (*ibid.*, p. 631). The philosophical system articulated by Sartre in *L'Être et le néant* (1943) is unquestionably its basis. However, Beauvoir's essay seeks in part to elaborate from that system her own existentialist *ethics*, a 'non-believer's morality' (Keefe, 1983, p. 79). A key facet of Beauvoir's speculation in part II of *Pyrrhus et Cinéas* is the theme of man's responsibility to and for *autrui*. This is a theme which is addressed extensively in *Le Sang des autres* and whose importance is announced at the start of Beauvoir's novel, in its Dostoievskian epigraph: 'Chacun est responsable de tout, devant tous'. Some initial discussion of Beauvoir's analysis of it in *Pyrrhus et Cinéas* will facilitate a more informed exploration of the treatment of human intersubjectivity and sociality offered in *Le Sang des autres*.

In her treatise, Beauvoir states that, as human beings, we exist ineluctably in a world of others ('Je me pare, je voyage, je bâtis parmi les hommes. Je ne peux vivre enfermé dans une tour d'ivoire'—*PC*, p. 111); others who constitute potentially antagonistic 'libertés étrangères' (*ibid.*, p. 110), but whose presence provides us with a (non-permanent) sense of meaningfulness. Consequently, our need of the other is

---

[1] Margaret A. Simons, 'Beauvoir and Sartre: the Philosophical Relationship', in *Yale French Studies*, 72 (1986), 165-79. This is a special issue devoted to Beauvoir.

immense ('nous avons besoin d'autrui pour que notre existence devienne fondée et nécessaire'—p. 96). More particularly, the other we need must be a *free* other, an equal ('il faut que j'aie devant moi des hommes qui soient libres'—p. 113)—because if the other is not possessed of 'liberté', he/she cannot confirm our projects, our transcendence*; cannot, in other words, stand guarantor to our own freedom. The 'liberté' of the other is, therefore, a matter of central, selfish concern to us, by virtue of its validating function ('Je lutterai donc pour que des hommes libres donnent à mes actes, à mes œuvres leur place nécessaire' —p. 112). It is also however a moral good; desirable in itself.

   In turning to other people for confirmation of our projects and our freedom, we impinge, inevitably, upon their being. Our need, in other words, indeed *the general fact of our existence,* inflects and affects their situation, even though as 'autrui' they remain radically *distinct* from us ('en tant que liberté, autrui est radicalement séparé de moi, aucun rapport ne peut etre créé de moi à cette pure intériorité [...]; ce qui me concerne, c'est la situation d'autrui, en tant que fondée par moi'(pp. 88-9). We cannot help but weigh heavily upon the other, forming a crucial part of 'la facticité* de sa situation'(p. 89). This, in turn, means that our 'rapport avec autrui' is and must be a relationship of *responsibility.* 'Le souci de [notre] rapport avec [autrui]' must be something that remains with us always, something for which we *take* responsibility; a responsibility that we have no right to ward off with specious excuses such as 'autrui est libre: [sa situation], c'est son affaire, non la mienne'(p. 89). We, as human beings, represent 'la fatalité qui pèse sur autrui'(p. 90). Consequently, for Beauvoir, we must shoulder and discharge, with a 'générosité lucide'(p. 84) the 'debt' to the other evoked in the Dostoievskian precept (p. 90) which is also cited at the start of *Le Sang des autres.* It is no good simply ignoring the existence of that debt. To choose to do nothing about it, passively, constitutes in actual fact a chosen mode of discharging it, and one that is morally reprehensible.

   How, then, should we positively assume our responsibility vis-à-vis the Other? Much of part II of *Pyrrhus et Cinéas* is devoted to a discussion of what Beauvoir calls *'ma* situation devant autrui'(p. 94), i.e. of the issue of our own liberty/ transcendence* and of the way the Other contributes to or curbs it. In consequence, the answer she provides to this question is rather sketchy (hence Keefe's sense of the 'flimsiness of her positive moral prescriptions' in *Pyrrhus et Cinéas'*— 1983, p. 79). *Le Sang des autres*, however, offers a far more focused examination of the issue of how we do—and how we *should*—relate to other people; particularly within the context of a period of collective crisis, when familiar rules and certainties disappear. With this in mind, we can turn back to that novel, and turn to a more detailed reading of it.

The ethics of blood-letting

In *La Force de l'âge*, Beauvoir describes the central protagonist of *Le Sang de autres* in the following terms: 'Mon nouveau héros, Jean Blomart, n'exigeait pas [...] de demeurer en face des autres le sujet unique; il refusait d'être pour eux un objet, intervenant dans leur existence avec la brutalité opaque des choses; son problème était de dépasser ce scandale en établissant avec eux des rapports translucides, de liberté à libertés'(p. 623). Her observations (couched in the somewhat rebarbative jargon of Sartrean existentialism) make it plain straight away that the moral dimension of *Le Sang des autres* is centred primarily around Blomart, and around the dynamic binding him to those people who come directly or indirectly into his orbit. In fact, Beauvoir exploits Blomart, and exploits the evolution of his dealings with *autrui*, in order ultimately to map out in her novel a kind of code for (co-) existence. Blomart's moral trajectory is tortuous and tortured, as the highly self-critical commentary of his 1940s' narrating persona reveals. By reconstructing that trajectory, and by teasing out its sequential development through an attentive reading of Blomart's narrative and of the asynchronic discontinuities and interruptions that punctuate it, the reader can extract from *Le Sang des autres* a Beauvoirian lesson in personal and social ethics. So what is that lesson? What form does Blomart's journey alongside and towards the Other—the vehicle for Beauvoir's moral speculation—actually take?

Blomart's moral evolution may be divided, somewhat over-schematically perhaps, into three stages:

i) a primordial or formative phase, which establishes other-related culpability as his dominant—indeed obsessive—characteristic;

ii) a phase of non-interventionism during which, in an effort to 'se garder pur'(**238**), he tries unsuccessfully to avoid confronting the 'malédiction originelle'(**194**) of our dangerous entanglement with the existence of other people;

and iii) a final phase that is characterized by radical action, by a commitment to the freedom of the individual/Other, and by a lucid acceptance of the price the pursuit of that freedom may elicit.

In each of these developmental stages, there is evidence of that imbrication of the personal and the political which Fallaize isolates as a key feature of *Le Sang des autres*. All three phases bear witness moreover to Blomart's profound engagement with the issue of our responsibility to *autrui*, an engagement which takes on a number of different forms in the course of his tale. They evolve as follows.

(i)   Blomart's lessons in loss

As a small boy, Jean Blomart, the son of a wealthy printer with a strong sense of class loyalty and hierarchy, is aware, almost from the cradle, that the protective, gilded cocoon he inhabits is haunted by something unspeakable, by a 'scandale' (**12**) compared to which the poverty and human wretchedness his socially-conscious mother occasionally allows him to glimpse is as nought. When he is eight, and a family servant loses her child, he discovers that the 'scandale' in question is existence itself, and the Sisyphean burden of culpability attendant upon it. The death of Louise's little boy, and the ineffectual comfort Jean and his mother offer her when they visit her shabby, exiguous flat, impel the youthful Blomart into a torment of grief and guilt: a guilt which is 'social, moral and existential' (Fallaize, p. 48) and which is evidenced by the following extract from *Le Sang des autres* (in which, as in a number of passages in the novel, culpability and eating difficulties are linked—see below, p. 56):

> Le petit de Louise est mort. En vain. Ce n'est pas mon
> malheur. *Ce n'est pas ma mort. Je ferme les yeux, je reste
> immobile, mais c'est de moi que je me souviens et sa mort
> entre dans ma vie: moi je n'entre pas dans sa mort.* Je me suis
> faufilé sous le piano, et dans mon lit j'ai pleuré jusqu'au
> sommeil à cause de cette chose qui avait coulé dans ma gorge
> avec le potage tiède, plus âcre que le remords: ma faute. La
> faute de sourire pendant que Louise pleurait, la faute de
> pleurer mes larmes et non les siennes. La faute d'être un
> autre. (18)

The primordial, critical moment in his trajectory recorded
here constitutes the point at which Blomart—still himself a
child—is afforded, on however instinctive a level, key
metaphysical insights into the nature of the self / other relation,
insights which underpin much of his subsequent development.
Confronted with the reality of human mortality and suffering,
Blomart intuits that he (and by extension every one of us) is
radically alienated from *autrui*, and that the 'original sin' of
our alienation—'la faute d'être un autre'—somehow
(paradoxically?) enmeshes our existence with that of other
people ('sa mort entre dans ma vie: moi je n'entre pas dans sa
mort'). It follows that our 'faute'—which, like the guilt it
engenders, is ineluctable ('elle est cet air même qui remplit mes
poumons, le sang qui coule dans mes veines'—12)—is
something we cannot help but take on board and act upon.

As he approaches adulthood, Blomart opts to act upon the
'original sin' of his alienation from the Other via a gesture of
social defiance / solidarity. Abandoning his family and class
(incarnated by the father who, in his willingness to engage
pragmatically with the corruption of the world and its ways
[20], is the object both of Jean's fear and of his contempt),
casting off the privileges that isolate him from the massed
ranks of common humanity, he becomes a worker amongst
other workers in the printing industry and, most importantly of
all, joins the communist party. At this point in his development,
Blomart is driven by an altruistic, idealistic impulse which,
moral and metaphysical in essence, manifests itself in the
specific guise of revolutionary political commitment. It is an
impulse which compels him to intervene actively in the world
and in the social situation of *autrui* in order that he might
realise that responsibility which, he senses, must be intrinsic to

human interaction. He is also motivated, however, as he
retrospectively realises, by a desire for self-exculpation, and by
a need to 'coïncider avec le choix qu'il faisait de lui-même' (*FA*,
p. 623). He is guided therefore—and this reminds us of the
character of Hugo Barine, the young bourgeois and would-be
communist created by Sartre in *Les Mains sales* (1948)—by a
not inconsiderable degree of self-interest ('Je ne pouvais pas
me tailler un sort dans un monde injuste; je voulais la justice.
Pour qui la voulais-je? pour les autres ou pour moi?'—**39**).

For a while, Blomart's other-related culpability is largely
expunged, so that he is less conscious of 'la faute d'être un
autre'—although he is haunted by the distress his actions cause
his mother, whose own sense of indebtedness to *autrui* and
liberal humanist propensity for 'bonnes œuvres'(**15**) do not
prevent her from denigrating radical *political* efforts to change
the social status quo ('Tout ce que condamnait son cœur et sa
raison, elle s'acharnait à le défendre: mon père, le mariage, le
capitalisme'—**21**). When, however, under his influence, the
adolescent poet Jacques Ledru joins the Party and is killed in the
course of a violent political demonstration, moral guilt
surfaces anew, and crystallises in Blomart into an enduring
feeling of criminality. After the cataclysmic loss of Jacques (an
event that occurs some time in the early 1930s), he re-orients
his position. Faced with the fact that direct (political)
involvement with / on behalf of *autrui*—which he has taken to
constitute a kind of moral imperative—is potentially fatal
('Comment aurait-il deviné qu'il était ce danger? *Dangereux
comme l'arbre inconscient qui répand au tournant de la route
son ombre sans poids*'—**27**), horrified at the consequences of his
own well-meaning conduct and choices ('Cette imprudence!
cette imprudence insensée!'—**22**), Blomart withdraws from
active political engagement, turning instead towards a non-
interventionist *modus operandi* that extends to his personal
dealings with other people. Jacques's death—a formative
experience that is as crucial for Blomart's evolution as the
death of Louise's baby—causes him to opt for what might be
described as an 'abstentionist' stance, which is not wholly
dissimilar to that of his mother (in the course of *Le Sang des
autres*, mother and son are in fact linked by a series of
identificatory parallels, which contribute to the reader's sense
of the intensity of their bond). This stance, Blomart believes,

will ensure that his effect and influence upon *autrui*—whose lot continues to be a central focus of his preoccupations—can only be anodine. However, as we shall see, his new position soon becomes untenable.

(ii) Detachment and its discontents

In the wake of the crisis of Jacques's death, Blomart's overwhelming desire is 'to be completely self-sufficient, to suppress all dangerous wishes and desires by suppressing all relations with others that cannot be controlled by his will' (Atack, p. 129). His abstentionism is complex. Like his commitment to communism, it combines altruism (because Blomart wishes to neutralize, via isolationism, the potential danger to the Other he has discerned within himself) and egocentrism (because it reflects a selfishly purist need no longer to compromise himself in / with the absurdity he perceives as intrinsic to the world around him). It is a position of protective, prudent responsibility, yet it rests upon a repudiation of the *active* responsibility to and for the Other which he has pursued hitherto (Blomart had previously deplored the 'prudence insensée'—21—characterizing his mother's conduct). On the level of the personal, Blomart's abstentionism manifests itself in his rejection of Hélène's attempts to seduce him and to insinuate herself into his life. In political terms, Blomart's refusal of involvement and activism impels him into an apolitical, pacifist syndicalism which, he hopes, will enable him to constitute for *autrui* a passive instrument of good instead of an invasive, fatal force:

> Après avoir quitté le parti, j'étais resté deux ans en léthargie; et puis peu à peu j'avais recommencé à m'occuper de la vie syndicale. Ce travail-là me semblait licite parce qu'il n'avait rien d'un travail politique; il était à une mesure humaine. Je n'avais pas à choisir pour autrui; je ne décidais rien; chaque membre du syndicat reconnaissait sa propre volonté dans la volonté collective; je n'exerçais aucune action sur le groupe auquel j'appartenais: je me bornais à être l'instrument à travers lequel il réalisait son existence [...]. **(77-8)**

In fact, Blomart's non-interventionist position proves to be unsustainable, and he finds himself forced to abandon both personal detachment and the political disengagement roundly condemned by his former comrades. As we shall see, he does so in the light of the palpable damage that issues (whether directly or indirectly) from his abstentionist stance, and in the face of an insurmountable truth, which is that to turn one's face against direct action and direct intervention in the lives of other people constitutes in itself a form of involvement or action, and one that can have significant—and deleterious—consequences.

Blomart is obliged at a relatively early stage in his story to confront the havoc wreaked by his refusal of interpersonal involvement, and to acknowledge that to remain detached from *autrui* does not necessarily protect and preserve the freedom of the Other. This is documented in chapter V, when he discovers that his rejection of Hélène has impelled her into a sexual misadventure with a 'sale type'(**123**), as a result of which she becomes pregnant and undergoes a backstreet abortion. The accusatory gaze Yvonne levels at Blomart (**122**) as she informs him of her friend's misfortunes—a gaze which is the very incarnation of that 'solidification et aliénation' of the human subject and his/her possibilities Sartre associates with the reifying, shaming 'regard de l'autre'(*EN*, p. 321)—and the subsequent spectacle of Hélène's pain and humiliation (the abortion scene is evoked in exceptionally graphic, grotesque detail) prove catalytic. They force Blomart to recognize that to abstain from involvement with another being, to ignore that being's demands for involvement—even out of a respect for her (his) liberty and integrity—does not in fact signify non-involvement but represents rather a mode of interpersonal engagement that inflicts harm. They oblige him to see that his abstentionist stance cannot justifiably be maintained in the face of an existence with which he is entangled, albeit against his will, and to which he owes a debt of responsibility:

> Je n'avais pas voulu entrer dans sa vie, j'avais fui, et ma fuite avait bouleversé sa vie. Je refusais d'agir sur son destin, et j'avais disposé d'elle [Hélène] aussi brutalement que par un vol. Tu souffrais à cause de moi, parce que j'existais. (**127**)

In consequence, until the advent of the war and the break with his lover which war provokes, he does enter into an emotional and sexual bond with Hélène. His (uneasy) commitment to her signals, on the level of the personal, an attempt to overcome his fear of inflecting the fate of the Other and to recuperate a position of active responsible involvement vis-à-vis *autrui*. Blomart's effort, and the release from moral guilt which it ought in theory to afford him, are, however, undermined almost immediately. One reason for this is the culpability inspired by the hurt his liaison with Hélène causes her ex-fiancé and his former mistress. The other, more significant reason is that Blomart does not (at this point) love Hélène wholeheartedly and authentically; he simply bends to her need of his love, and complies with it. As he himself senses, this transforms his attempt to guarantee her happiness into an exercise in manipulation, and into an infringement rather than a consolidation of her liberty ('rester inerte, docile devant sa volonté, c'était encore créer de ma seule autorité une situation qu'elle ne pouvait que subir. Elle était là, ligotée par mes mains dociles, enfermée dans un amour sans joie'—**167**). Both factors ensure that the affair cannot in fact generate that relation of reciprocity, of freedom to freedom with other people which, Beauvoir suggests, comes to be Blomart's ideal. Its demise— which follows Hélène's attempt to have Blomart released from active army duties, and which does not in fact prove permanent—is consequently unsurprising.

Blomart's emergence from self-imposed political abstinence proves to be a more tardy—if ultimately a more successful— affair. This is because his desire to maintain a position of non-violent political neutrality has been embedded deep within him by the guilt Jacques's death engenders. Before we examine more closely Blomart's adherence to, and eventual rejection of, a neutral, anti-interventionist stance, it is useful briefly to establish the broader politico-historical context in which that stance can be situated. In the section of *Les Intellectuels en France* entitled 'Sous le signe du Front populaire 1934-1938' (pp. 93-113), Ory and Sirinelli address the issue of how the intelligentsia of the French Left (amongst whom, clearly, we may class Blomart) 'placed' themselves politically in the prewar period, specifically with regard to international events. They explain that while the growth of fascism impelled committed communists (like Beauvoir's Paul, for instance) to adopt a unified, anti-pacifist position, based upon the certainty that embracing pacifist non-interventionism meant turning a blind eye to, indeed encouraging, the spread of the fascist menace in Europe, the majority of their fellow-travellers on the Left believed that war must be avoided at all cost:

> Face à deux puissances fascistes dont l'expansionnisme se précise de jour en jour, le pacifisme intégral peut en effet passer pour une prime à l'agression. Cette conviction soude l'intelligentsia communiste, mais ne rallie qu'une partie des socialisants, radicaux et sans-parti, et sans doute une minorité d'eux, si puissants sont encore sur leur esprit l'horreur de la guerre et le scepticisme devant les discours visant à la justifier au nom du 'Droit'. (Ory and Sirinelli, p. 110)

This phenomenon casts light on Blomart's political/ethical evolution in the central section of *Le Sang des autres*.

In chapters III and V (set in the mid-1930s), it becomes clear: i) that, in his post-communist, syndicalist phase, Blomart is determined not to use the authority he enjoys within his trade union in order to advocate any kind of politically-motivated strike, or to make any gesture of active solidarity with the anti-fascist movement born in France in the early 1930s in response to events in Europe and within France itself; ii) that this determination reflects his moral sense that his debt to *autrui* can best be discharged by an avoidance of political choices whose effects may prove fatal:

> Moi aussi, je souhaitais de toutes mes forces la déroute des Maures de Franco; mais ce vœu solitaire, cet intime tressaillement de ma chair, je me reconnaissais pas le droit d'en tirer une volonté qui s'imposerait à mes camarades. [...] Je savais à jamais qu'on ne peut pas cerner les limites d'un acte, ce qu'on est en train de faire, on ne peut pas le prévoir. Plus jamais je ne courrais ce risque insensé. (**146**)

Gradually, however, the pressures of History—manifested through a series of interpellations to commitment and via the 'concrete unpalatable evidence of the consequences of abstentionism'(Fallaize, p. 50)—cause him to eschew non-interventionism.

Blomart is the recipient of two appeals to action, both of which are documented in chapter V (in many ways the fulcrum of *Le Sang des autres*). The first is delivered by Madeleine, who, disgusted by the head-in-the-sand attitude of the socialist

powers-that-be in France to the horrors of the Civil War in
Spain, asks Jean to help her cross the border and rally to the
Republican cause, and urges him to involve himself and his
union in the fight against Franco and fascism:

> —Les salauds! me dit-elle. Ils les laisseront crever sans leur
> envoyer aucun secours.
> —Tu sais, l'intervention ça pourrait être lourd de
> conséquences.
> —Pourquoi n'essayez-vous pas une grève? peut-être que
> Blum céderait.
> —Je ne veux pas de grève politique, dis-je. (146)[2]

The second challenge to Blomart's pacifist apoliticism comes
from Blumenfeld, a Jewish-Austrian socialist deeply committed
to the fight against Hitler. Blumenfeld's accounts of Austrian
Nazi activities prior to the *Anschluss*—accounts which are part
of his attempt to convince Blomart that it is his duty to use his
syndicalist influence in order to shift French public opinion
towards an acceptance of active resistance to Nazism, even if
that acceptance brings war in its wake—unsettle Jean deeply.
However, the self-interrogation and guilt provoked by
Blumenfeld's arguments (guilt manifested once again by an
inability to eat: 'la bouchée que j'avalais me resta au travers de
la gorge'—151) still fail to impel Blomart into interventionism,
because he cannot shake off the conviction that interventionism
(on his part) puts the Other (here, the workers of France) at
risk:

---

2 The situation Madeleine is describing / deploring here is as follows. In July 1936,
Franco, backed by the army, overturned the legitimate, Republican government of
Spain—a Popular Front, like that of France. Italy and Germany supported Franco. In
the face of appeals for help from the displaced Spanish government, Blum, the premier
of the Front populaire, yielded to the opposition to intervention prevalent amongst the
Radicals on the Left, and to his fear of being perceived by the French Right to be
dragging France, out of ideological solidarity with Spanish socialists, into a situation
which might lead to war. Consequently, he adopted, along with the government of
England, a policy of non-interventionism. As Antoine Prost explains, this did not go
down well with other elements on the French Left: 'La non-intervention est mal
acceptée par les ouvriers français, qui réclament des avions et des canons pour l'Espagne.
Elle crée des conflits dans le Front populaire, les communistes lui étant hostiles. Le
compromis consiste à fermer les yeux sur la contrebande avec l'Espagne républicaine,
voire à l'organiser, sans pour autant équilibrer l'intervention italo-allemande' (*Petite
histoire de la France au XXe siècle* [Paris: Colin, 1979], p. 41). The fact that Blum's
government *did* in fact turn a blind eye to the issue of 'contrebande' elicited
denunciations from those on the French Right who were pro-fascist.

> Derrière les Pyrénées, les travailleurs d'Espagne tombaient
> sous les balles fascistes, mais pouvais-je racheter leur sang au
> prix de vies françaises, au prix d'une seule vie qui ne fût pas
> la mienne? Les Juifs crevaient comme des mouches dans des
> camps de concentration, mais avais-je le droit d'échanger
> leurs cadavres contre les corps innocents des paysans de
> France? Je pouvais payer avec mon corps, avec mon sang;
> mais les autres hommes n'étaient pas une monnaie à mon
> usage [...]. (**154**)

For the duration of chapters V and VII, Blomart continues to deflect, albeit with increasing anguish, the call to commitment. Because he cannot entertain the possibility of being responsible for the sacrifice of any human life, even if that sacrifice will save many more lives, he uneasily maintains his pro-pacifist position. As Beauvoir explains, he clings to the belief that 'les hommes ne sont pas des unités qu'on peut additionner, multiplier, soustraire; ils n'entrent dans aucune équation parce que leurs existences sont incommensurables; en sacrifier un pour sauver dix, c'est consentir à l'absurde'(*FA*, p. 264). The inevitable advent of War modifies his stance dramatically. Initially, war appears simply to offer Blomart a welcome respite from the need to choose, as an individual, between neutrality and interventionism. Soldiering, even killing, is mechanistic, the good/evil divide becomes clear-cut ('Une nécessité clémente commandait chacun de ses actes'—**229**) and, absorbed by the collectivism of army life, he succumbs to the 'tentation de se fondre dans l'universel'(*JG*, p. 366). Subsequently, however, war and its consequences force him to the conclusion that his refusal to opt for anti-fascist commitment/intervention, however well-intentioned, has constituted 'a kind of intervention which maintains an intolerable situation' (Atack, p. 126) and that his 'prudence insensée'(**238**) has involved a derogation of his responsibility to *autrui*.

This inculpatory 'évidence' is brought home to him when he discovers that his fellow pacifist, Gauthier, has chosen to collaborate with the German forces now occupying France. In the face of it, he opts —in true 'boy's own paper' style, which reminds us once again of the degree of resemblance binding Blomart and Sartre's anarchistic Hugo Barine—for action and active resistance: 'Il faut des actes bien visibles [...]. Des trains de munitions qui sautent, des hôtels réquisitionnés qui explosent. Il faut que les Français se sentent encore en guerre' (243). He is aware that this interventionist course may involve him in further harm to and 'crimes' against *autrui*, but has come to view the guilt of abstentionism as the more unacceptable burden. He is, in any case, weary of the endless, inner moral turmoil to which he is subject and which History has rendered superfluous ('À la fin, la défaite, l'occupation l'acculaient à une décision: par-delà tous les raisonnements et tous les calculs, il découvraient en lui des refus et des impératifs absolus. Il renonçait à démêler le nœud gordien: il tranchait'— *FA*, p. 624). The extent to which his wartime stance involves a radical reversal of his earlier moral position regarding the (non-) justifiability of spilling the blood of his countrymen is made clear during an argument he has with the men to whom he turns for financial backing in chapter IX. This discussion, illuminating as it does the extreme point to which Blomart's engagement with the issue of responsibility to / for the Other has by this stage led him, merits quotation *in extenso:*

> —Ce sont des représailles que j'escompte, dit-il [Blomart].
> Pour que la politique de collaboration soit impossible, pour que la France ne s'endorme pas dans la paix, il faut que le sang français coule.
> —Ainsi, vous laisseriez fusiller sans remords des innocents? dit Parmentier.
> —J'ai appris de cette guerre que le sang qu'on épargne est aussi inexpiable que le sang qu'on fait verser, dit Blomart. *Pas de grève politique. Je ne pousserai pas mon pays à la guerre. Et nous voilà. Assez. Assez. Cette prudence insensée.* Pensez à toutes ces vies que notre résistance sauvera peut-être.
> Ils se turent longtemps.
> —Mais si notre effort avorte, dit Parmentier, nous nous retrouverons chargés de crimes inutiles.
> —Sans doute, dit Blomart. De toute façon on était toujours criminel, mais ces deux-là ne le savaient pas, le crime leur faisait peur [...]. (244)

(iii) Commitment, resistance and self-reproach

The history books inform us that, by mid-1941, certain (primarily communist-led) sections of the French Résistance

were going on the offensive.[3] Terrorist attacks against the
German forces who controlled all of France save for the Vichy-
run 'zone libre' were increased—the first German serviceman
was shot in the Métro on 21 August, and there were
derailments, grenade explosions, etc. These attacks were
greeted by German reprisals, which began in late 1941.
Generally speaking, the victims of such reprisals were
themselves 'résistants' (a key exception here is the 800-strong
population of Oradour-sur-Glane, 642 of whom were
massacred by the Germans on 10 June 1944). In *L'Après-vivre*,
Serge Doubrovsky records a conversation with his elderly
uncle, a former member of the Resistance and a Jew, in which
the old man recalls how, after he had been taken prisoner by
the Germans, an SS officer who shared his love of modern
poetry was sufficiently 'charitable' to put him not in 'la cabane
aux juifs' (which would have meant immediate deportation)
but rather in 'la cabane aux résistants': 'là on ne tue pas
aussitôt, on massacre à la carte, selon les besoins en otages'.[4]

The issue of *représailles* and of the sacrifice of French blood
is a central feature of the final chapters of Beauvoir's novel.
When Blomart and his (non-aligned) group embark upon their
resistance activities, his new-found belief that 'toute monnaie
était bonne même celle-ci: le sang des autres'(**245**; cf. **154**) is
translated into reality. Blomart and the cell of which he is
leader (a cell which includes, somewhat improbably, almost
every other character in Beauvoir's novel, even Blomart *père*,
with whom Jean is reconciled by virtue of their mutual, if
differently motivated, investment in anti-fascism) perform acts
of sabotage and violence against the Germans and their
collaborators; acts which certainly risk bringing reprisals in
their wake and which are justified for Blomart by the kind of
moral argument he offers Parmentier in chapter IX. This
provides a context for the fact that, in the 'narrative present' of

---

[3] For an account of the ways in which the various political parties in France
positioned themselves vis-à-vis Resistance activity, see the chapter entitled 'Partis
politiques et syndicats' in Henri Michel's *Histoire de la Résistance en France* (Paris:
PUF, 1972), pp. 34-40. Michel explains that 'les Communistes œuvrèrent dans les deux
zones [nord et sud]. Toute une presse régionale, autour de *l'Humanité*, diffusa leur
propagande. À la suite de leur reconstitution, incontestablement, le nombre de sabotages
augmenta sensiblement: nombre d'entre eux payèrent leur action par une exécution ou une
déportation' (p. 39).

[4] Serge Doubrovsky, *L'Après-vivre* (Paris: Grasset, 1994), p. 162.

Le Sang des autres, Blomart must decide whether or not to give the go-ahead to a bombing aimed at destroying the anti-Bolshevik exhibition. In view of his history, we might suppose the outcome of his decision to be automatic. Surprisingly, however, until the very last page of the novel, he cannot pronounce his verdict. His failure to do so is provoked by two key factors.

The first is the spectacle of the dying Hélène, at whose bedside Blomart keeps an anguished vigil throughout his 'dark night of the soul'. Hélène finally accepts commitment, joins Blomart's resistance group and wins (seemingly in direct consequence) the authentic love she has desired, but she is fatally wounded in the course of a foray which he has instigated and in which he has reluctantly involved her. As he watches the life ebbing from her body, Blomart's anxieties about the morality and the perils of impinging upon the existence of the Other, and about the 'fatal' character of his own choices and interventions—anxieties which are never wholly expunged, but with which he has reached an accomodation—are revived. The second (less crucial) factor which contributes to his crisis is a red poster that appears on the white walls of the Métro in the aftermath of an earlier act of violent sabotage in which, unusually, Blomart has been personally involved. The poster announces that twelve hostages have been shot in revenge for this particular bombing, and that twelve more will die unless the culprits give themselves up. The feelings of personal culpability it arouses in Blomart (feelings which provoke, once again, eating-related difficulties [289] and which are intensified by the denunciation of the bombers he hears on the lips of his beloved mother, a non-interventionist to the end), like the sight of Hélène's moribund form, make it almost impossible for him to utter the words that will set in train a new attack and provoke a new set of reprisals against yet more innocent French prisoners. Eventually, however, he does elect to sanction the attack, and to accept the burden of searing remorse attendant upon his choice.

Blomart's resolution of his final dilemma is preceded (and facilitated?) by exculpatory assurances which, even as she loses the tenuous hold on life that remains to her, Hélène generously offers her lover. She insists that her devotion to him, her entry into the resistance and her death itself have been a function of her *own* will and freedom, that the over-arching responsibility for her choices and destiny which he imputes to himself is ill-founded, because she has remained mistress of her own fate. Hélène's observations conveniently release Blomart from the remorse provoked by his belief that his intervention in her life and liberty has made of him her murderer, the obstacle/stone against which her existence has foundered. They work retroactively also, we sense, to attenuate his guilt at the infringement of her freedom he undoubtedly did perpetrate during the period of their 'phoney love', and to heal the anguish caused him by the role his political example has played in Jacques's death.

It may be the case that Hélène's 'absolution' allows Blomart to start to reconcile himself with the fresh impingement upon the existence of the Other which inheres to the act of political sabotage (and to its after-effects) whose authorization he defers as he watches at her bedside. However, any relief or release from culpability afforded by his lover's words can only be temporary. Blomart must confront the fact that his relation to Hélène's death and his role vis-à-vis the hostage-deaths that will follow his sanctioning of a fresh bombing campaign are not of the same order. He may not be morally responsible for the demise of his mistress, but saying yes to Laurent will, without doubt, make him into an assassin:

> Il regarda le lit. Pour toi, [je n'ai été] rien qu'une pierre innocente: tu avais choisi. Ceux qu'on fusillera demain n'ont pas choisi: je suis le roc qui les écrase; je n'échapperai pas à la malédiction: à jamais je resterai pour eux un autre, à jamais je serai pour eux la force aveugle de la fatalité, à jamais séparé d'eux (310).

In the light of this, we need to ask ourselves what causes Blomart finally to opt for the affirmative response he makes to his comrades' demands for a decision; demands which, present at the beginning and the conclusion of *Le Sang des autres*, provide the structural framework for his narrative. How is it that, faced with the concrete reality that is Hélène's corpse, he can accept as a necessary evil the expenditure of lives that his 'je suis d'accord' will engender?

As Beauvoir observes in *La Force de l'âge*, Blomart's decision not to depart from the course of violence upon which he has embarked is neither designed nor destined to afford him ease of mind. It derives in part from his sense that abandoning armed struggle prematurely will mean that for those French citizens whose lives have already been lost to Fascism—Hélène, the 'douze otages' of the red poster—death will have been a vain, absurd obscenity. It rests more importantly upon Blomart's realisation that in a world where 'crime' is always somehow attendant upon our dealings with other people, so that a clear conscience is impossible, and where the freedom of the individual (and of the collectivity) is and must be the supreme good, actions liable to bring that freedom about—actions aimed at the overthrow of murderous political régimes, for instance—must be pursued, regardless of their localized consequences and of the anguish responsibility for them may engender in their perpetrators. This is the sense of the metaphysical 'mission statement' Blomart articulates at the very end of *Le Sang des autres:* a statement which marks the climax of his journey towards the Other and towards a commitment to liberty / responsibility that is lucid, situation-based and pragmatic: 'Mais que seulement je m'emploie à défendre ce bien suprême qui rend innocents et vains toutes les pierres et tous les rocs, ce bien qui sauve chaque homme de tous les autres et de moi-même: la liberté [...]' (**310**). Blomart's final reflections—which reiterate his vision of himself as a 'roc' obliterating the life of the hostage-victims—would seem to suggest, moreover, that if we choose to fight for the freedom of the individual, and, in the course of that fight, are obliged to sacrifice *particular* individuals, the 'bien suprême' that is our ideal will, if realised, bring with it some measure of absolution.

Ethical Doppelgänger

The moral trajectory which Beauvoir traces, via Blomart, in *Le Sang des autres* illuminates amongst other things that 'rapport du social au métaphysique' which, according to her *Journal de guerre* (p. 366), she sought to sketch out in her second novel. It signals also an effort on Beauvoir's part to

move away from the kind of solipsistic theorization of the self /
other relation contained in Sartre's *L'Être et le néant* and
exemplified in her own *L'Invitée:* a theorization ('la théorie des
consciences ennemies'—Gennari, p. 33) which focuses on the
intersubjective, individual dimension of that relation at the
expense of the collective / sociopolitical, and stresses its
fundamental antagonism. Clearly, the ethical lesson embodied
in Blomart's *péripéties* requires synthesis and comment. It is
worth pausing briefly, however, to consider the extent to
which other characters in *Le Sang des autres* contribute to the
development of the novel's moral dimension. One of the most
obvious things to say about the majority of these characters
(Madame Blomart is the central exception here) is that they
come in the end, in one way or another, to support Blomart and
to support and adhere to the course and cause he finally
chooses, reinforcing thereby the 'message' (and the
absolutionary aspect) of the end of *Le Sang des autres*.

More particularly, Beauvoir makes a somewhat formulaic
use of specific members of Blomart's entourage in order to
delineate his moral journey more clearly. Fallaize notes, for
instance, the over-schematic opposition Beauvoir establishes
between Blomart's parents, remarking that at the beginning of
the novel, 'the dialectic set up between the mother and the
father, the mother representing a recoil from action, the guilt-
induced desire to retain as much purity as possible by doing
nothing, and the father representing the nauseous pragmatics
of action, sets the pattern of Blomart's subsequent oscillations'
(p. 48). His movement towards a total commitment to the
Other and to (political) freedom—a movement which, as we
have seen, is consolidated by his encounter with History—is
paralleled in minor mode by that of two other characters:
Marcel and Hélène. Both display in the prewar period different
forms of self-absorption which mirror the (neurotic, bourgeois)
self-preoccupation that Denise Ledru imputes to Blomart as
late as chapter XI (**285**), but which are in no way compensated
by the altruism that drives Beauvoir's hero from the outset.
Hélène's egotism manifests itself via a narcissistic inability to
concern herself with, or even to perceive, the connectedness of
her individual lot and that of humanity as a whole ('Dans sa
jeunesse, Hélène [...] se croyait radicalement détachée de la
collectivité; elle ne se souciait que de son salut personnel'—*FA*,

p. 624). Marcel's lack of solidarity is indicated by the solipsistic, self-oriented creativity, the 'pure' art requiring no audience to validate it, which he makes his goal (and which may be read as the aesthetic equivalent of the politico-personal isolationism Blomart pursues after Jacques's death). However, Hélène's experiences during the Occupation and Marcel's discovery, after he is captured by the Germans, of the value of an art which creates bonds with and between his fellow prisoners and of the utter unpalatability of fascism, impel both into active resistance and into a belated solidarity with *autrui* which echoes Blomart's own. Hélène's trajectory bears some striking similarities—and dissimilarities—to that of her lover. When war breaks out she, unlike Blomart, endeavours to avoid facing up to History, to her own involvement in it and to the call to solidarity it imposes ('Les yeux secs, elle regardait passer les hommes et les chevaux, les tanks, les canons étrangers, elle regardait passer l'Histoire qui n'était pas la sienne'—256). However, like Blomart, she is subject to a series of (visual) stimuli which constitute appeals to involvement and responsibility, stimuli that make it less and less easy for her to maintain her self-interested detachment. This detachment represents, indubitably, a consequence of the pain her break with Blomart has caused her—and indicates also, perhaps, an unconscious perception on her part that History is a 'male' affair?

The first of these stimuli is the spectacle of the everyday casualties of war: a mother and her starving child exhausted by the flight from Paris that follows the German invasion (260). The child's eyes seem to reproach Hélène for her indifference to the suffering that is going on all around her, and she is discomfited by the message they convey. The second is a hostage poster recording another anti-resistance atrocity by the Germans; an atrocity whose implication for / of herself Hélène strives, unsuccessfully, to minimize by dismissing it as one of those necessities of History which do not touch her (273). The third is a (shame-inducing) revelation of her *être-pour-autrui*: a vision of self-as-collaborator afforded by a glimpse of her reflection in a nightclub mirror as she dances in the arms of a German officer, surrounded by a luxury that forms an obscene counterpoint to the deprivation her fellow countrymen must endure under the Occupation (275). The fourth is the anti-

Jewish *rafle* she witnesses, in the course of which Yvonne and her mother narrowly escape arrest and Hélène must confront the suffering of another mother and her child (the 'Ruth' whose memory haunts her fading consciousness as she loses hold on life), separated by the French *miliciens* who are abetting the deportations (**292-7**).

All of these stimuli cause Hélène to understand that she cannot view the oppression of others that is occurring around her as divorced from her own (female) existence, or choose not to combat it actively, since to do so is to choose to keep it in place. Consequently, she joins Blomart's cell, assuming that commitment to *autrui* which her lover has long advocated and whose necessity war finally enables her to perceive. Terry Keefe points out that 'her new stance appears, characteristically, to be more of a reaction to individual distress than a carefully thought-out choice'(1983, p. 166). It is undoubtedly presented as such by Beauvoir, and it worth noting that in *Le Sang des autres*—an *œuvre de jeunesse* by a woman who was subsequently to become a / the leading voice of French feminism—politics and informed political choices are represented squarely (and problematically) as gendered, and as the province of men. The fact that Hélène's movement towards anti-fascist commitment is shown to be instinctive rather than 'engagé' is not the only instance of this phenomenon. Denise's efforts to express deeply-held political beliefs are dismissed by Blomart (and by Beauvoir?) as pompous and self-interested ('Je détestais l'entendre vaticiner sur le destin du monde; elle essayait de se libérer ainsi du souci de sa propre vie'—**159**), while Madeleine's ill-fated trip to Spain (having burnt her foot in a basin of boiling oil, she spends six months in bed before being repatriated to France) is presented as the result of girlish enthusiasm and folly (**147**). In *Le Deuxième Sexe* (1949), Beauvoir argues that if woman is imprisoned 'au cœur de sa subjectivité' and lacks a (political) 'prise sur le monde' (*DS*, p. 547), a proclivity for action and activism, etc, this is a function of her invidious situation under patriarchy as opposed to a natural phenomenon. *Le Sang des autres*, however, a narrative which, admittedly, was not 'framed' by Beauvoir as a feminist production and which privileges a *male* voice / perspective—is haunted by the alarming implication that women and politics simply do not mix.

Beauvoir's moral messages

Linda Singer describes Beauvoir's philosophical writing as 'the voice of the ethics of otherness'(p. 232). What, in summary, are the ethical arguments offered in the fictional *Le Sang des autres*? In essence, there are three of them:

i) As Beauvoir observes in *La Force de l'âge*, and as Blomart grasps precociously, we must accept and assume the debt our entanglement with the Other imposes. Alienation may be our original condition and sin, but 'bon gré mal gré, nous intervenons dans des destins étrangers et [...] nous devons assumer cette responsabilité'(*FA*, p. 700).

ii) Our assumption of responsibility for the Other, and for our intervention in his/her 'destin', must never *invade* the liberty of *autrui* (as Blomart's efforts to take Hélène's existence into his charge and to 'lui construire un faux bonheur'(see *JG*, p. 368) do in the middle section of the novel, by virtue of the dissimulatory arrogance that lies at their heart). It must, rather, take the form, on the interpersonal *and* the political/collective levels, of an ongoing, active *commitment* to human freedom and to the establishment of conditions permitting 'des rapports translucides de liberté à libertés'.

iii) Any action is morally justifiable if it combats oppression and engenders the freedom of the individual/individuals. However, the paradox here, as Blomart's hostage dilemma illustrates and as Beauvoir argues in her philosophical essay *Pour une morale de l'ambiguïté* (1947), is that 'aucune action ne peut se faire pour l'homme sans se faire aussitôt contre les hommes'(p. 143), and that the quest for (collective) freedom may in certain circumstances involve the sacrifice of individual lives and liberties.

Le Sang des autres constitutes a compelling tale, in which contextualization makes abstract ethical problems vivid and real. To what extent, though, does the moral message of Beauvoir's novel prove convincing? Individual readers must clearly decide this for themselves. It is certainly possible, in spite of the careful arguments set up in chapter IX and especially at the end of *Le Sang des autres*, to find it hard to reconcile Beauvoir's / Blomart's patent defence of the 'valeur singulière et irréductible'(*PMA*, p. 166) of the individual and his / her liberty on the one hand, and Blomart's evident invasion and violation, on the other, of the existence / freedom of 'ceux qu'on fusillera demain'. Readers may feel, too, that the sustained debate around the ineluctability and necessity of our responsibility vis-à-vis the Other contained in *Le Sang des autres* is weakened by Blomart's quasi-pathological obsession with this issue and (especially) by the improbably excessive guilt his dealings with *autrui* arouse in him. It is tempting to speculate as to the source of the exaggerated culpability he manifests. In *La Force de l'âge*, Beauvoir remarks that she attributed to Blomart some of her own childhood sentiments and emotions—most notably an anxiety at enjoying social privilege at the expense of others—but that these particular biographical borrowings in no way justify the intense feeling of guilt that dominates and poisons his life (p. 627); a feeling which she herself acknowledges as extreme.

Beauvoir's establishment here of a link between her own problems of conscience and those of her vocalically homonymic creation Blomart is not unilluminating. Beauvoir was a member of Sartre's (largely ineffectual, short-lived) resistance group 'Socialisme et Liberté'; however, she staged a play and published her first novel during the Occupation (a cultural collaboration avoided by many), signed a teachers' declaration stating that she was not Jewish, and was linked moreover with René Delange, the editor of the collaborationist literary journal *Commœdia*, who used his influence to get her a job in radio (the Germans controlled the French media).[5] It is not inconceivable that the disquiet and self-inculpation Beauvoir's compromises during the war years may have inspired in her filtered into the psychology of her character, particularly in those sections of her novel which focus on his failure to discharge his debt to the Other by standing up to fascism.

In *La Force de l'âge*, Beauvoir ruefully endorses Maurice Blanchot's negative reading (in *La Part du feu*) of *Le Sang des autres*, a reading which dismisses her text as a 'roman à thèse'

---

[5] For an account of Beauvoir's and Sartre's implications in collaborationism, see Deirdre Bair, *Simone de Beauvoir: a Biography* (London: Jonathan Cape, 1990), especially pp. 258-60; 279.

impoverished by its dogged progress towards a 'conclusion univoque, réductible en maximes et en concepts'(*FA*, p. 627). How justified is Beauvoir's self-flagellation here? To what extent *is Le Sang des autres* a *roman à thèse* bent primarily, or even uniquely, on delivering an unambiguous moral lesson? Supposing, moreover, that Beauvoir's text does merit this generic designation, must we, regardless of Beauvoir's own view of the matter, consider it as necessarily impoverishing? In *Authoritarian Fictions*, Susan Suleiman defines the *roman à thèse* as 'a novel written in the realistic mode (that is, based on an aesthetic of verisimilitude and representation), which signals itself to the reader as primarily didactic in intent, seeking to demonstrate the validity of a political, philosophical or religious doctrine'.[6] She makes the point too that 'whether its thesis is conservative or radical, defending the *status quo* or calling for its abolition, the *roman à thèse* is essentially an authoritarian genre: it appeals to the need for certaintly, stability and unity that is one of the elements of the human psyche' (Suleiman, p. 10).

In *Le Sang des autres*, Beauvoir does not make the mistake of offering, in 'authoritarian' mode, black-and-white answers to the moral questions she raises, or indeed of providing any foreclosing resolution of these questions without having first acknowledged the complexities intrinsic to them. Blomart's eventual, radical conclusions concerning the centrality of freedom and the justifiability of acts of violence perpetrated in its cause are, for instance, subject to a series of hard-hitting counter-arguments. These counter-arguments are vehicled not only by the comments of characters such as Parmentier, with his fear of committing 'crimes inutiles'(**244**), and Madame Blomart—who, as Yolanda Patterson remarks, 'represents a kind of collective conscience forcing [her son and his generation] to think hard about the taking of any human life, be it that of the enemy or of countrymen' (1986, p. 92)—but also by Blomart's own pro-pacifist reflections and observations in the central section of the novel. Even his defence of the necessity of responsibility and solidarity—which is far less contentious than his advocacy of violence—is called into question by Hélène in chapter II.

---

[6] Susan R. Suleiman, *Authoritarian Fictions: The Novel as Ideological Genre* (Princeton University Press, 1983), p. 7.

That said, the didactic dimension of *Le Sang des autres* is unmistakable and primordial. Beauvoir's novel *is* a text with a decidedly 'ideological' emphasis / message, but is this such a bad thing? As Suleiman argues, critical readers need to be wary of dismissing the ideological novel as simply propagandist, or of perceiving its exemplars, as Beauvoir herself evidently came to do, as unliterary in their 'didactisme'(see *FA*, p. 629). Suleiman suggests that while the *roman à thèse* is often criticized for its reliance on the outmoded notion that literature can and ought to perform a communicative function,[7] it should in fact remain of interest to contemporary readers: i) because it represents a 'particularly clear manifestation of the realist *and* didactic impulse that lies at the heart of the novel, and that persisted as a foundation for it until relatively recently' (Suleiman, p. 18); and ii) because the contestation of modernist conceptions of literature that it incarnates can encourage readers to reflect, productively, upon what writing and representation are 'about'.

Suleiman's comments are helpful to Beauvoir's readers in that they encourage us to detach ourselves from the unduly negative retrospective assessment of *Le Sang des autres* which Beauvoir herself chose to make in 1960: an assessment which, ironically, is announced within the boundaries of her novel itself, by the negative critique of *Denise's* novel that is uttered by Blomart himself in chapter VI ('Vous expliquez trop, dit Jean. Vous ne montrez rien. Vous avez quelque chose à dire et vous ne vous souciez pas beaucoup de la manière de le dire'—181). We need to bear in mind, too, that *Le Sang des autres*, whilst undoubtedly offering an (existentialist) lesson in personal and social ethics, is not reducible to a string of metaphysical and moral arguments transmuted mechanistically into fiction. Beauvoir's text provides, amongst other things, a compelling account of the intricacies of emotional and desiring interaction;

---

[7] As Suleiman points out, 'modern criticism has been tremendously wary of any literary work that "means to say something" (that has a message), and of any critic or reader who reads literature as an "attempt to say something"—who reads it for its "message". The Sartrean dream of transparent language [...] has been replaced, in contemporary avant-garde criticsm, by Mallarmé's dream of language as a mirror of itself'(*Authoritarian Fictions*, p. 18). Another way of putting the same point is to say that modern criticism prefers, in literature, the self-referential text to the work that aims for referentiality, i.e. claims to represent and to offer a message about something—society, the human individual etc.—that is outside itself, in the real.

an account which belies her self-condemnatory description of *Le Sang des autres* as a morality tale whose heroes lack psychological depth and constitute mere cyphers for a range of ethical stances: cyphers devoid of 'racines vivantes'(*FA*, p. 627). With this in mind, let us now turn to the 'love story' element of Beauvoir's novel, which will provide the focus of the next part of this study.

Chapter Two

Death and the maiden:
the perils of desire

In her illuminating analysis of Beauvoir's late novella *La Femme rompue*, Toril Moi suggests that readers need to distinguish between: i) the 'authorial interpretation' they are *invited* to make of Beauvoir's short story—and of its heroine—by its author's explicit observations and intentions regarding her tale; and ii) the 'readerly' reading engendered by 'what one might call the intentionality of the text'(1990, p. 62). For Moi, these interpretations are in fact in tension with each other. The first is subtended by the hostility which Beauvoir palpably feels towards Monique, the central protagonist of *La Femme rompue;* the second, by the identificatory sympathy Monique (arguably) inspires in Beauvoir's (female) readership.

Likewise, two rather different—if not oppositional—readings may be made of the treatment of love offered by *Le Sang des autres*. The first of these may be considered to be an 'authorial', or 'sanctioned', reading of the novel, in so far as it mirrors the directive commentary on *Le Sang des autres* provided by Beauvoir in *La Force de l'âge* and also parallels elements of her description of the Woman in Love contained in the 'Justifications' section of Volume Two of *Le Deuxième Sexe*. The second interpretation evolves, arguably, from what Moi terms 'the "logic" of the text': a logic predicated upon 'the [reader's] feeling that *this* is what the various elements [of the story] add up to, whether the author knows it or not' (*ibid.*). It offers, moreover, a more intricate vision of what, in terms of desiring interaction, is 'going on' in *Le Sang des autres* than that furnished by Beauvoir's authorial and autobiographical interpretation. If we adopt this latter interpretative strategy, we find confirmation of Martha Evans's contention that the 'peremptory reading of her own texts' which Beauvoir insinuates into her autobiographical works contrives 'to rationalize the confusions of her [...] fictions and thus to preclude the reader from facing the trouble that is there' (p. 70).

Authorial directives

The 'authorial' interpretation which we are invited to make of the tale of love that Beauvoir weaves in *Le Sang des autres* rests upon existentialist ontology. It relates moreover to the kind of analysis of gender relations which Beauvoir came to produce in the late 1940s. It is worth pausing briefly to recall certain of the premises of such an analysis. Lack of space obviously precludes a detailed account or critique of them:

> i) Women—social Others *par excellence*—are constructed socioculturally, by patriarchy, as 'êtres inessentiels'. 'Enfermées dans la sphère du relatif'(*DS*, p. 547), their intrinsic human liberty is restricted. Scandalously, they are born free and autonomous but, unlike men, are impelled by their situation into the un-freedom of alterity and immanence*; into, in other words, the 'urge toward passivity, toward the being of a thing'.[1]

> ii) The female 'subject' may seek, in consequence, to manifest/ pursue her transcendence,* not via a series of ever-changing choices and projects—full access to these is effectively denied her by her 'condition'—but rather via the (male/superior') Other: 'ce que rêvera la femme qui n'a pas étouffé sa revendication d'être humain, c'est de dépasser son être vers un de ces êtres [hommes] supérieurs, c'est de s'unir, se confondre avec le sujet souverain; il n'y a pas pour elle d'autre issue que de se perdre, corps et âme en celui qu'on désigne comme l'absolu, l'essentiel' (*DS*, p. 547).

> iii) For a man, Love is an activity, not a definitive goal or project. For (heterosexual) women, on the other hand, it may represent the 'be-all and end-all', and may involve them in 'une totale démission au profit d'un maître'(*ibid.*).

How does all of this illuminate *Le Sang des autres*? On the one hand, in contrast to the sluggish, promiscuous Madeleine and the doggedly devoted Denise, whose efforts at creativity fail, and whose troubled, parasitic love for Marcel Ledru

---

[1] Jo-Ann Pilardi, 'Female Eroticism in the Works of Simone de Beauvoir', in Jeffner Allen and Iris Marion Young (eds.), *The Thinking Muse: Feminism and Modern French Philosophy* (Indiana University Press, 1989), p. 21.

almost drives her into madness, Hélène Bertrand is presented
by her creator as possessing a marked capacity—and taste—
for independence and liberty. We must not forget that both
Madeleine and Denise do endeavour to realise an active
project, a 'prise sur le monde', via political and later resistance
activism. However, this fact does not appear—for Beauvoir, at
least—to mitigate against her characters' fundamentally
immanent* status, or to make them Hélène's equals in terms of
enterprise and energy (see Leighton, p. 125). Madeleine
emerges as incarnating bodily passivity, whilst Denise, for
much if not all of the novel's duration, seeks to live and define
herself vicariously, through Marcel and his art. This must
constitute what Blomart terms her 'secrète disgrâce'(82).

Hélène's (admirably) independent nature is intimated by a
number of the descriptions we are given of her early on in *Le
Sang des autres*, descriptions which evoke, for instance, her
vibrant personality, her sprightliness, her persistent pursuit of
happiness, the transcendence*-related 'ardeur de vie qui la
jetait vers l'avenir'(89), and so on. It is highlighted, somewhat
comically, by the account the reader is offered, in chapter II, of
the enthusiasm she feels for her stolen bicycle, a bicycle whose
'air fier et libre' is clearly employed by Beauvoir as an indicator
of its mistress's own free-spirited temperament. Evidently,
then, she is no representative of that 'incapacité à être, à créer,
à vivre', of that 'complexe d'échec, vécu en pleine conscience'
which Geneviève Gennari pertinently associates with a
number of Beauvoirian heroines (p. 68). None the less, Hélène
succumbs all too rapidly to the self-mutilatory, 'romantic'
desire for justification in and via the loving gaze of the male
desiring Other (or 'témoin'), which Beauvoir imputes in *Le
Deuxième Sexe* to the immanent* 'amoureuse'. Increasingly
she is imbued with a sense of the meaninglessness and the
'ennui' (55-6) of the existence that is hers in a world from which
God has disappeared: 'Quand j'étais petite, je croyais en Dieu
[...,] alors il me semblait que je *devais* exister. C'était une
nécessité'(92). Convinced of the impossibility of self-
sufficiency, she turns to Blomart—who, unlike her fiancé Paul
seems to incarnate the combination of authority and distance
her narcissistic masochism requires of a lover—for
confirmation of her selfhood, of her existence:

> Je ne vais pas le revoir avant des jours, et des jours. Et lui ne
> pense pas qu'il ne me verra pas; il ne pense pas qu'il ne
> m'aime pas. Tout est plein autour de lui. Je n'existe pas pour
> lui. Je n'existe pas du tout. (101)

Unfortunately for Hélène, however, that confirmation is long in coming, a fact which she endeavours, stubbornly, to gloss over. For the greater part of their liaison, even after Blomart enters into an affair and, subsequently, an engagement with her, he cannot love her authentically and cannot therefore 'justify' her being as she hopes and desires. He is unable to do so partly because he cannot overcome his own, avowedly cold-blooded 'nature ingrate, du genre constipé' (134), and partly—more importantly—because, whilst he succumbs to her charm, he cannot wholeheartedly 'esteem' Hélène. Ironically, his lack of esteem derives, to a degree, precisely from her girlish deification of him, a deification which he finds both deplorable and invasive ('C'était avec ma propre chair qu'elle composait ce héros dont tous les souvenirs, les pensées, les sourires étaient miens mais dans lequel je ne me reconnaissais pas'—*ibid.*). When, however, Hélène (having lost Jean thanks to her selfish desire to protect him from war and to preserve him for herself) comes belatedly to shrug off self-serving individualism and to embrace solidarity and resistance activism—achieving concomitantly a 'prise sur le monde' and a more authentic mode of existence than that permitted by the non-project of devotion to another being—Love is, finally, her reward. When, in other words, she emerges from her blameworthy, solipsistic indifference to *autrui*—another source of the alienating 'manque d'estime' Blomart feels for her—the confirmatory self-justification intrinsic to the love of the Other comes her way. His emotional and affective commitment is won by Hélène even as it ceases to constitute the wholly central, overvalued desideratum it previously represented for her, and ironically, just before she dies. As Beauvoir explains in *La Force de l'âge*:

> Blomart, quand elle le rencontrait, la fascinait, à cause de la
> force et des certitudes qu'elle lui prêtait; elle quémandait un
> amour qui lui eût apporté, croyait-elle, une absolue
> justification d'elle-même; mais il se dérobait. [...] Dans la
> générosité de la camaraderie et de l'action, elle finissait par

conquérir cette reconnaissance—au sens hégélien du mot—
qui sauve les hommes de l'immanence* et de la contingence*.
(*FA*, p. 625).

This citation confirms that the 'reading' of the love
dimension of *Le Sang des autres* offered in the preceding
section of this discussion—a reading which revolves around
the notion that women, even strongly individualistic ones, fall
easily into the trap of making love and the lover the sole site or
source of their 'meaning'—derives squarely from the
autocritical, 'authorial' account of her novel provided by
Beauvoir in her autobiography. It is, moreover, the reading
which is implicitly favoured and foregrounded by the narrative
force of that novel, Jean Blomart. A number of the
retrospective comments made by his older, narrating persona
(see **158**; **197**) actively stress, for instance, Hélène's desire to be
confirmed and made meaningful by his love (a phenomenon
which blurs the boundaries between Blomart's intradiegetic
narrative voice and the autobiographical voice of his creator,
Beauvoir). It is, however, a reading that contrives not to take
account of many of the complexities intrinsic to the tale of love
that is told, one that fails to explain adequately the complicated
nature and underlying tensions of Blomart's own 'attachment'
to Hélène. This will provide the central focus of our second,
'readerly' interpretation of love in *Le Sang des autres*.

In chapter V, just as Blomart is busily warding off Hélène's
demands for total and exclusive Love and is reflecting, more
than a little self-congratulatorily, on his constitutional *inability*
to offer her anything more than a lukewarm admixture of
'tendresse' and 'indifférence', he is stopped in his tracks by
Denise's observation that: 'Vous ne *voulez* pas l'aimer' (**158**).
This remark is illuminating in that it suggests that Blomart's
refusal to engage completely with Hélène is a function not of
any essential emotional incapacity on his part, but rather of his
will, of his non-desire to love. In the light of this, we need to
ask ourselves why it is that Beauvoir's hero will not (as
opposed to cannot) love the woman with whom he is
nevertheless intimately and physically entangled, and how it is
that he comes in the end to do so just before she loses her life.

Before he embarks upon his relationship with Hélène (and,
for a while, in coincidence with it), Blomart regularly sleeps
with Madeleine. However, his recollections of that liaison

suggest that it has presented certain difficulties, of an erotic nature: 'Avec Madeleine, nous faisions l'amour en silence et presque toujours dans la nuit: elle subissait le trouble et le plaisir avec une espèce d'horreur comme elle subissait les voix et les regards et même le visage immobile des choses; quand je la caressais, je me sentais toujours criminel'(137). On the face of it, Blomart seems here simply to be describing the sexual discomfiture of his lover. However, it is possible—indeed tempting—to view his remarks as projective, and as indicative of his own 'horreur' and unease, an unease which is stimulated by the proximity of Madeleine's passive, sexualised, womanly body and which surfaces elsewhere in the text (83). In *L'Être et le néant*, Sartre presents the experience of desire as profoundly disruptive of that consciousness* which marks us out as human creatures capable of transcendence*. With his customary misogyny, he implies, moreover, that if desire constitutes a kind of trap for consciousness*, it is a trap laid somehow by the immanent* woman:

> C'est qu'on ne désire pas une femme en se tenant tout entier hors du désir, le désir me *compromet,* je suis complice de mon désir. [...] Il n'est pour chacun que de consulter son expérience: on sait que dans le désir sexuel la conscience est comme empâtée; il semble qu'on se laisse envahir par la facticité*, qu'on cesse de la fuir et qu'on glisse vers un consentiment *passif* au désir. (*EN*, p. 457).

Given the nature of Blomart's memories of sex with Madeleine, it seems likely that he is not entirely immune to the distaste for feminine flesh, and to the fear of the lure of facticity* incarnated by that flesh, implied by Sartre's observations. This, we might suppose, may in turn account for the barrier Blomart establishes—quite deliberately—between himself and Hélène. However, Blomart asserts his belief that Hélène's love-making does not impel either herself or him into that state of submerged consciousness* which Sartre deplores, and that this is because *her* female desire (unlike Madeleine's) preserves her—and his—freedom, contriving thereby not to 'compromise' either of them:

> Tu ne te sentais pas la proie d'une fatalité honteuse; au milieu des élans les plus passionnés, quelque chose dans ta

> voix, dans ton sourire disait: «C'est parce que j'y consens.»
> Par cette constance à te déclarer libre, tu me mettais en paix
> avec moi-même. (137)

We need, consequently, to find another way of explaining
Blomart's 'réticences' vis-à-vis Hélène. The issue here,
evidently, is not—or is not simply—a fear on his part of contact
with, and contamination by, her desiring body.

We have already encountered evidence of the strength of
Blomart's identificatory attachment to his mother. Madame
Blomart, for all her political and existential contradictions, is
the model from which Jean derives his sense of altruism; she is
also, frequently, the arbiter of his decisions (**167**; **175**). There are
numerous indications in *Le Sang des autres* that Jean's
attachment to her is in fact founded, from its inception and
enduringly, not simply upon filial devotion but also upon an
intensity of unactualised Desire—hence Fallaize's contention
that Blomart is trapped for much of the novel in the grip of an
unresolved Oedipus complex which places 'a stranglehold on
his emotions'(p. 58). Clues to the profoundly eroticised nature
of Blomart's infantile bond with his maternal parent abound in
chapter I, where the adult Blomart evokes (and retroactively
enjoys?) his boyhood, fetishistic delight at the sight of his
mother's shoes and her naked, exposed shoulders (**17-18**). The
presence in the parental home of his authoritarian father
constituted, patently, a powerful, 'castratory' disincentive to
the young Jean's Oedipal, incestuous impulses. In spite of his
childish efforts to dismiss Blomart senior as a minor figurant
within his mother's emotional universe, and to construct him,
jealously, as 'cet homme qu'elle n'aimait pas'(**33**), we sense
that the paternal obstacle against erotic mother-love
incarnated by M. Blomart represented an interdictory force
with which his son could not easily refuse to comply.
Nevertheless, Jean's libidinal attachment to his mother,
repressed, tacit and taboo as it undoubtedly becomes, is never
fully extinguished. In chapter VII, the mature Blomart reveals
himself—to Mme Blomart's evident distress—to be fascinated
still by her footwear (**176-7**), and, as late as chapter XI, we find
him longing to be tucked up in bed and kissed goodnight by
Mummy (**289**).

Clearly, then, Blomart's Oedipal feelings survive long
beyond their natural, infantile timespan, and, arguably, are

never worked through, even though they come to be muted.
This, in turn, offers us insights into why it is that Beauvoir's
hero is so persistently dogged by excessive feelings of guilt.
Guilt, Freud suggests, is intimately bound up with the super-
ego, whose role, within the unconscious, is 'assimilable à celui
d'un juge ou d'un censeur à l'égard du moi'.[2] The super-ego is
formed at that moment at which a child resolves his or her
Oedipus complex (i.e. around the age of three to five years).
Because Blomart patently fails properly to achieve Oedipal
resolution—complicating, thereby, the process via which the
super-ego comes into being—his capacity for culpability is,
arguably, intensified to a pathological degree.

Blomart's relationship with Mme Blomart is, in essence, one
which can 'legally' admit emotional and sentimental love but
which must (and yet ultimately fails to) preclude desire. What is
the consequence, for his adult *vie affective*, of his intense idyll
with his mother? How might the complexities of that highly
ambivalent relationship engender and inflect his emotionally
impoverished union with Hélène? In addressing these
questions, it is worth considering the hypothesis that Blomart's
mother-fixation compels him to form, in adulthood, liaisons
which are the antithesis of his bond with Mme Blomart,
liaisons which involve women who are decidedly unmaternal,
with whom Jean can consequently enjoy the erotic desire/
pleasure that has hitherto been (Oedipally) forbidden him but
who do not impel him into Love (Love being reserved for the
Mother alone). Is this hypothesis borne out by the 'facts' of
Beauvoir's text? It certainly appears to be, as far as Blomart's
dealings with Hélène are concerned; so much so, in fact, that
Hélène would seem on the surface to constitute the perfect
sexual companion for Blomart. On the one hand, as we know,
he can and does feel desire for her. His desire is triggered,
straight away, by her charmingly childlike mien and
demeanour, and by her glowing, seductive adolescent
physique: in other words by traits which, insistently stressed in
Beauvoir's text, transform Hélène into an ideal—because non-
maternal and consequently non-transgressive—object of erotic
attraction for Blomart. On the other hand, Hélène slips easily,
if unwillingly, into the role of she-whom-Blomart-will-not-

---

[2] J. Laplanche and J.-B. Pontalis, *Vocabulaire de la psychanalyse* (Paris: PUF,
1967), p. 471.

love. The dynamics of their bond—dynamics which she herself upholds—make it perfectly possible for him to maintain his self-imposed ban on love; for love to be uniquely on her side.

Unfortunately for Blomart, the neat erotic equilibrium sketched out above—an equilibrium which is based upon the necessary, indeed time-honoured, separation of the (loved) 'femme / mère' and the (desired, desirable) 'femme / objet érotique'—fails to transpire in and as a result of his relationship with Hélène. This may explain the anguish that regularly haunts him before and during his sexual involvement with his lover. The problem is that Hélène is not, after all, as unmotherly as all that. She is not only linked by identificatory factors of class and taste to Mme Blomart (hence the latter's approval of her) but is presented from the start, for all her self-absorption, as possessing distinctly nurturing, 'maternal' qualities. When we first meet her, she is offering sweets to a small boy who comes into her parents' chocolate shop; subsequently (71); during a strike, she feeds Blomart himself. Hélène's problematic blurring of the oppositional feminine categorizations on which Blomart relies in order to be able to desire actively and openly is announced (49) early on by the link she herself establishes between her desire to 'séduire' and her compulsion to force-feed (*gaver*) the male Other (a link which recalls, once again, the omnipresent food-as-problem topos).

Blomart's response to that blurring is to seek incessantly to infantilize Hélène, to 'dematernalize' her. Her incipient 'motherliness' threatens his desiring system, and threatens *him*, so he endeavours to defuse it by framing her endlessly as a (desirable) 'petite fille'. However, the menace intrinsic to the maternal dimension of Hélène's character—a menace which, we sense, is the spur to Blomart's refusal, for a long time, to involve himself sexually with her at all—persists. It arouses in Blomart what is, undoubtedly, a deeply-buried, unarticulated, powerful death wish. This death wish is directed against Hélène—who, intermittently, is but should not be Mother—and is (paradoxically) somehow 'matricidal'. Belonging as it does to the 'other scene' of the Unconscious, it is manifest in *Le Sang des autres* in the obsessive reiteration of a key structuring figure of the text; that motif of red-plus-white which connotes violence and murder (viz. the red hostage poster on the white-tiled wall of the Métro) and which, tellingly, is repeatedly associated with Hélène's clothing (see **71**; **86**; **125**). It is as if the child-woman who feeds him, whose unexpected 'maternalization' disrupts Blomart's self-protective divorce of the familial / motherly and the sexual, must pay for her nurturing, must bleed and die.

Blomart's unconscious need to realize his hidden, 'matricidal' compulsion (a compulsion which may conceivably connect to the complexities of his possessive bond with Mme Blomart as well as to Hélène) becomes intense during the nightmarish abortion episode in chapter V. In this episode—in which the red / white murder motif recurs with unnatural frequency—Hélène, 'avec cette chose dans son ventre'(**125**), is provisionally and horrifyingly more of a mother than usual. She remains so until she considerately voids her uterus, metamorphosing herself once again into a 'si petite fille'(**126**) that Blomart can subsequently initiate the sexual affair on which he embarks with her later in the chapter. The powerful lure which the possibility of (pseudo-) matricide exerts upon him explains why he is so morbidly fascinated here by the pain he witnesses Hélène experiencing as she loses her foetus, and by the 'sang rouge de femme'(**129**) her body disgorges. It explains, too, Blomart's curious failure to prevent the potentially life-threatening use, by the aged *faiseuse d'anges*, of a pair of dirty scissors to facilitate Hélène's termination; a failure which he endeavours, unconvincingly, to attribute to a loss of nerve on his part (**130**). It may even account, on some level, for the violent desire to strangle Hélène ('j'aurais voulu serrer mes mains autour de son cou jusqu'à ce qu'il n'y ait plus *rien* entre mes mains'—**231**) which overwhelms Jean in chapter IX after he discovers that, in classical 'maternal' mode, she has hooked him back from the front, cutting him off from the male camaraderie of army life and from the space of mother-related independence and individuation to which soldiering had briefly offered him access ('Avec tant de joie il avait endossé la capote couleur de terre, et fait raser les cheveux trop riches, trop serrés qu'il tenait de sa mère'—**230**).

Hélène's demise at the end of the novel can also, arguably, be read as a kind of actualization of Blomart's murderous, pseudo-matricidal impulses. It is after all he who—albeit reluctantly—sends her on her fatal mission, thereby sacrificing *her* life-blood to *his* cause and provoking a death which,

Fallaize argues, 'functions as a liberating force for Blomart, allowing him to project forward into a future which is not for [Hélène]' (p. 63). This particular interpretation of the climax of Beauvoir's tale cannot help, if we endorse it, but cause us to revise our sense of the validity of the 'absolution' Blomart is offered by Hélène in chapter XIII. As a reading, it may seem far-fetched. More pertinently, it may appear to be unreconcilable with the fact that by the time Hélène meets her fate at the hands of the Germans, Blomart is genuinely and fully in love with her at last. There is not necessarily any contradiction here, however. It may be the case that Beauvoir's hero *can* only love Hélène when he knows that she risks encountering the death he has unconsciously willed for and wished upon her, i.e. after she joins the Resistance (in chapter XII). It may precisely be the spectre of her loss, and, more particularly, the sight of the 'cadavre' her (maternal/adolescent) body is becoming, which enable him finally to offer her the total, intense devotion hitherto reserved for the Mother.

In Gide's *L'Immoraliste*—a male-authored, male-narrated (semi-autobiographical) tale in which another mother-proxy repeatedly bleeds for and because of a man who fails to love her properly—the male hero's love, argues Naomi Segal, is born out of his unstated delight at seeing the woman's life drain away.[3] Michel's devotion to Marceline, Segal suggests—a devotion which intensifies as she sickens—is the concomitant of his 'matricidal' obliteration of her (an obliteration manifest, for Segal, in a whole series of other French, male-authored *récits* of the eighteenth and nineteenth centuries). A similar phenomenon may perhaps provide a clue to the emotional reversal Blomart effects in the concluding chapters of *Le Sang des autres*. If we accept that it does, then it is hard not to wonder at Beauvoir's exploitation, in her novel, of such a very 'masculine' ending. It is worth recalling here that the motif of matricide does, in fact, surface elsewhere in Beauvoir's multi-faceted *œuvre*. It may be viewed less as a male, misogynistic 'borrowing' than as the signal of a personal obsession: a signal

---

[3] Naomi Segal, *Narcissus and Echo: Women in the French 'récit'* (Manchester University Press, 1988), pp. 160-75. It is worth noting in passing that when Beauvoir was planning the composition of *Le Sang des autres*, Gide was one of the models she had in mind as a basis for Blomart.

which reveals, according to Toril Moi, Beauvoir's own, deep-rooted need to mark 'an absolute *triumph* over and *liberation* from the realm of the mother' (1994, p. 120). Whether this phenomenon helps us to perceive Beauvoir's staging of Blomart's displacedly maternal / matricidal degradation of Hélène as any less unpalatable remains, of course, open to question.

Establishing Hélène's relation to the love / desire dynamic that is so central to Blomart's emotional equilibrium proves to be less than straightforward. This is because the reader's access to her sentiments is constrained by the modalities of Beauvoir's narrative technique. As the introduction to this discussion indicated, in the even-numbered chapters of *Le Sang des autres* an external, third-person narrating voice is predominantly employed—albeit one which offers insights into the workings of Beauvoir's heroine's mind and emotions, and which is interrupted on occasion by more 'intimate' sequences of direct speech / thought, first-person *discours immédiat* or *monologue intérieur*.[4] We are afforded, therefore, a far less unmediated purchase on Hélène's consciousness than on that of her lover, which is openly and insistently on display in the odd-numbered, predominantly first-person-oriented chapters of the text, chapters which are weightier than the 'Hélène' chapters and constitute a 'frame' for them (hence Fallaize's point that in *Le Sang des autres*, 'the female discourse is absorbed into the male'—p. 63). One result of this is that in Beauvoir's novel, rather as in a number of the male-authored, exclusively male-narrated *récits* analysed by Segal in *Narcissus and Echo*, 'the woman's desire is barely audible', and can consequently be '[translated] in the ears of the hero into what he wants to hear' (p. 11). Key evidence of this particular form of male / female occultation is provided in chapter V. The account we are offered here of Hélène's 'transcendent'* experience of freedom-in-desire (**137**) is not focused through her, as we might expect it to be, but is instead narrated by Jean (becoming, in consequence, less objectively credible and more

---

[4] According to Gérard Genette, 'dans le discours immédiat, le narrateur s'efface et le personnage se substitue à lui' (*Figures III* [Paris: Seuil, 1972], p. 194). Édouard Dujardin defines the *monologue intérieur* as a 'discours sans auditeur et non prononcé par lequel un personnage exprime sa pensée la plus intime', *Le Monologue intérieur* (Paris: Messein, 1931), p. 59.

'wishful' than the reader might at first have supposed). We do not hear Hélène herself giving voice and credibility to this experience. All we have is Blomart's perspective on it.

This is not to say, however, that Hélène's relationship to desire remains wholly obscure(d) in *Le Sang des autres*. There are at least three occasions, in those chapters of the novel where she is the centre of consciousness, on which the nature of that relationship is conveyed to the reader, and conveyed in a way that jars with Blomart's 'reading' of it. There is, for example, the moment in chapter IV at which Hélène (at this point still engaged to Paul) almost succumbs to her fiancé's efforts to seduce her, and to an intensity of desire that is presented as 'une pâle vapeur sucrée', a 'charme qui la métamorphosait doucement en plante'(**103**):

> ... elle respira avec effort; elle avait peine à respirer, elle s'enfonçait au cœur de la nuit, elle perdait pied; les yeux clos, paralysée par ces rets de soie brûlante, il lui semblait que plus jamais elle ne remonterait à la surface du monde, qu'elle resterait à jamais enfermée dans ces ténèbres gluantes, à jamais une obscure et flasque méduse couchée sur un lit d'orties enchantées. (**104**)

The threatened eclipse of conscious selfhood, the desiring descent into fleshly, sticky facticity, and the disquiet inspired by that descent which are all conveyed in this (highly 'Sartrean') passage are twice echoed elsewhere in *Le Sang des autres*, at moments when Hélène is led to reflect upon the erotic bond that links her not to Paul, but to the more seductive, 'superior' Blomart, with whom she is in love. On both of these occasions, the blood motif, which plays so primordial a role in Beauvoir's novel, resurfaces. In chapter VI, Hélène becomes intensely aware, as Blomart approaches the bed where she lies waiting for him, of 'une brume ardente [qui] courait dans ses veines; ardente, aveuglante'(**192**), of a fogging of her entire being which transforms her into 'plus rien qu'un corps aveugle' (*ibid.*). In chapter VIII, she is drawn to focus upon the 'tornade brûlante qui séchait le sang dans ses veines'(**224**). As in the 'orties enchantées' passage in chapter IV, with its images of glutinous, vegetal darkness, these extracts and the metaphors employed within them connote danger and (self-)destruction as much as passion. Their implication is that for Hélène, the experience of desire is not after all, exclusively, a liberatory epiphany—not even when it is shared with the beloved, and with a lover who perceives it so to be. It involves rather a consciousness*-destroying 'trouble', and a kind of 'abdication honteuse' of the self (DS, p. 166) which is not precluded by Hélène's evident capacity for sensuality. This recalls Beauvoir's highly pessimistic account in Le Deuxième Sexe of the alienated nature of the female sexual condition under patriarchy: an account which suggests, in essence, that as long as women are culturally positioned as slaves to the species and as erotic objects they will never be able to enjoy their sexuality fully and unproblematically.[5]

If desire is, then, something which Hélène experiences, however instinctively, as a trap, we need to ask ourselves how it is that in the central section of Le Sang des autres she can enter into, and persist with, a sexual relation with Blomart, a relation which even he comes to perceive as troubled:

> Nos baisers, nos caresses avaient vite perdu la limpidité heureuse des premiers jours. Souvent des ombres passaient sur son visage et tandis que je l'embrassais elle fermait les yeux avec un air de souffrance; parfois au milieu d'une étreinte, elle se dégageait brusquement. (140)

It is hard not to conclude that her need to elicit narcissistically gratificatory recognition-via-Love, and to elicit it from a man possessed of the requisite degree of 'prestige'(DS, p. 554), is so strong that she will pay any price to realize it, even if that price involves accepting the compromise of selfhood which desire apparently imposes upon her (Blomart, as we saw above, seems less prone to such degradation). Readers may choose to speculate as to the existence of other, less conscious sources of Hélène's ambiguous relation to sexuality (a relation whose nature and development are plunged into obscurity after the end of chapter VIII). However, Beauvoir's text, on this particular subject, remains too elusive to justify devoting space here to considerations of this kind.

---

[5] There is insufficient space here to gloss in detail Beauvoir's analysis of feminine sexual alienation. For a highly lucid account of it, which draws attention, inter alia, to the fact that beneath Beauvoir's indictments of what patriarchy does to / makes of the female body lurks evidence of a palpable, personal ('Sartrean') disgust for that body on Beauvoir's own part, see the chapter 'Ambiguous Women' in Moi (1994), pp. 148-78.

Readerly perspectives

The bipartite analysis of Beauvoir's representation of love and desire in *Le Sang des autres* offered in the preceding section of this discussion focuses more or less exclusively on the textual data provided by and within her fiction. It may appear, moreover, to be well-nigh exhaustive. For the reader who is prepared to look *beyond* the textual boundaries of Beauvoir's novel and to take into account the role which extratextual, personal factors may have played in the evolution of the desiring scenario it stages, there is, however, more to be said. The temptation to read *Le Sang des autres* from a biographical standpoint, and to treat it as a *roman à clé*, is compelling. The adoption of an approach of this kind becomes all the more appealing in view of the fact that in recent years, after the posthumous publication by Sylvie Le Bon de Beauvoir of the (highly revelatory) *Journal de guerre* and *Lettres à Sartre*, Beauvoir criticism has taken on a distinctly personal(ised) tenor—or, to put it more accurately, has become even more, or differently, author-oriented. As Toril Moi rightly points out, it has long been common practice for 'many critics first [to] reduce every text by Beauvoir to her own persona'(1990, p. 28). Biographical criticism is an enterprise which, although highly seductive, is fraught with problems. Not least amongst these is its speculative, prurient character, and its tacit foregrounding of the notion that, within the realm of literary analysis, the extratextual must take precedence over the textual, so that 'tout est acceptable, pourvu que l'œuvre puisse être mise en rapport avec *autre chose* qu'elle-même'.[6] Readers of the present study must bear these points in mind as they peruse what follows.

In *La Force de l'âge*, Beauvoir states that if the character of Hélène Bertrand 'comes alive' more effectively than her co-actors, and has 'plus de sang' than the other protagonists of *Le Sang des autres*, this is because 'j'y ai mis davantage de moi-même'(*FA*, p. 628). Hélène and her creator are certainly bound by identificatory ties, which are most in evidence in chapters VIII and X. In these episodes, the experiences to which

---

[6] Roland Barthes, 'Les Deux Critiques', in *Essais critiques* (Paris: Seuil, 1964), pp. 246-51 [p. 251].

Beauvoir's heroine must submit during her illicit visit to the army camp at Pecquigny and her flight out of and journey back to Paris in the wake of the German invasion mirror almost exactly Beauvoir's own wartime adventures, ones that are transcribed in her *Lettres à Sartre II* (pp. 130-41), in her *Journal de guerre* (pp. 298-325) and in *La Force de l'âge* (pp. 504-520). However—as elements of this discussion have already indicated—it is Blomart rather than his lover who may be considered to 'be' Beauvoir in *Le Sang des autres*. It is to her male protagonist that Beauvoir attributes, for instance, her enduring, guilt-ridden anxieties about mortality. The shocking, initiatory 'encounter with death' (and with social injustice) which Blomart experiences as a boy when he learns of the fate of Louise's baby parallels a childhood incident recorded, quasi-obsessively, in Beauvoir's autobiographical *Mémoires d'une jeune fille rangée* (pp. 6-7; 135; 183-4), a text in which, as in *Le Sang des autres*, the death of the Other is represented as a catalytic and highly formative phenomenon. Blomart is, moreover, the site within Beauvoir's novel of a whole series of perceptions, sentiments and instincts—relating, for example, to women and love, to the mother, and to the female body—which are overtly present or hinted at elsewhere in Beauvoir's *œuvre* and which are indubitably her own.

Most importantly, Blomart's attitude to Hélène's persistent courtship of him is founded squarely on Beauvoir's personal reaction, charted in her autobiographical writings, to the behaviour of her former pupil, Nathalie Sorokine—from whom, in turn, Beauvoir borrows a whole range of traits that are imputed to Hélène (including bicycle thievery and abrasive charm). Fallaize notes these facts, commenting (not entirely accurately) that 'in so far as the Blomart-Hélène relationship has an autobiographical base, it echoes the structure not of the Beauvoir-Sartre model but of the encounter which Beauvoir had during Sartre's absence in the war with Nathalie Sorokine, to whom [her] novel is dedicated' (p. 63). All of this suggests that what Beauvoir does in *Le Sang des autres* is to effect a kind of textual division of her own persona, which results in the creation of two biographically-inflected self-projections: a 'major-self' (Blomart) and a 'minor-self' (Hélène) who is also an Other (Sorokine) and who, ultimately, is textually suppressed, both existentially (because she dies) and narratively. What is the reader to make of this 'schizophrenic' phenomenon? What light does it shed on the dynamic of desire chronicled in, and on the more general development of, Beauvoir's novel?

In order to address these questions, we need first to look more closely at the nature of the author's relationship with Nathalie Sorokine. Their bond was a complex one. In *La Force de l'âge*, Sorokine—renamed Lise Oblanoff—is presented as motivated by a classic, teacher-related schoolgirl crush, as something of a pest—albeit a touchingly devoted one (*FA*, p. 399)—and as a being on the periphery of Beauvoir's existence. However, as Emma Wilson indicates in her illuminating reading of Beauvoir's letters and war diary,[7] the relationship between mentor and student was far more complicated, and far more intense, than Beauvoir's 'official' autobiography admits. It was, for a start, a sexual liaison upon which Beauvoir, in spite of her other lesbian experiences, embarked with some trepidation ('Je savais devoir coucher avec [Sorokine] et je craignais des déchaînements passionnés, mais elle a été toute plaisante et légère et imprévue comme à son ordinaire'—*JG*, p. 231 [5 janvier 1940]). It was also, as Wilson convincingly argues, a relationship which Beauvoir exploited in order to reactivate the hierarchised emotional and sexual paradigm governing her bond with Sartre (see *LS II*, pp. 57-8 [19 janvier 1940]; Bair, pp. 191; 200), but to reactivate it in such a way that *she* gained access to the dominant, loverly role which had, hitherto, been Sartre's, thereby usurping the position of (male) privilege occupied and enjoyed by her long-time companion (and competitor?). Finally and most importantly, for all Beauvoir's pursuit of control vis-à-vis desire / Sorokine, it was a highly-charged erotic tie which, as Wilson puts it, 'continually slip[ped] out of Beauvoir's control, [which] makes Beauvoir's journal all the more interesting to read since the text of order, veracity and control is cross-cut with anxiety, indecision and desire'. Evidence of this latter point is amply supplied by Beauvoir's war diary, in which Beauvoir's controlled and controlling assertions that her feelings for Sorokine involved 'pas une ombre de passionnel

---

[7] 'Daughters and Desire: Simone de Beauvoir's *Journal de guerre*', in Terry Keefe and Edmund Smyth (eds.), *Autobiography and the Existential Self: Studies in Modern French Writing* (Liverpool University Press, 1994), pp. 83-98.

[...] mais une immense tendresse et estime'(*JG*, p. 241 [13 janvier 1940]) are juxtaposed with more telling articulations of desire and disquiet, of the following type: 'elle ne me demande pas de l'aimer passionnément et je prends bien garde cette fois à ne pas le lui laisser croire, mais elle voudrait que je tienne à elle. J'y tiens vraiment et quand elle me quitte je reste toute secouée' (*JG*, p. 254 [24 janvier 1940]).

As indicated above, Beauvoir's personal, projective input into *Le Sang des autres* was considerable. The insights into her bond with Nathalie Sorokine and, more generally, into her wartime *vie affective* which we are afforded by her *Journal de guerre* (and by Wilson's excellent analysis of it) help us to 'read' that input in a way which would not otherwise have been possible. For one thing, these insights illuminate the textual 'self-masculinization' upon which Beauvoir undoubtedly embarks in *Le Sang des autres* by dint of imputing her own emotions and experiences to her chief male protagonist. If a strategy of Sartre-oriented displacement did subtend Beauvoir's emotional life during the period when she was involving herself with Sorokine and was beginning to plan and write *Le Sang des autres*—and it seems likely that this was the case—then her creation within her novel of a fictional self or double who occupies a *male* subject position, and a position of acknowledged authority, becomes comprehensible. It can be interpreted, clearly, as a facet within, or contributory factor to, a broader pattern of (unconscious) gender-role usurpation into which Beauvoir was propelled by the intricacies—and rivalries—of her relationship with her 'petit compagnon'. What may appear less immediately comprehensible is why Beauvoir should allow Hélène, her second textual alter ego or minor / female self, to be 'killed off' by her major, male, authority-self (Blomart). However, this too can be explained in terms of the emotional and sexual situation in which Beauvoir found herself in the early 1940s. That situation—eroticised, lesbianised and 'slippery' as it came to be—was evidently deeply troubling for Beauvoir, so troubling, in fact, that in 'Carnet VI' of her *Journal de guerre* she felt impelled to comment: 'J'aurais voulu être seule et l'idée d'avoir à passer quatre heures avec Sorokine m'a levé le cœur'(*JG*, p. 338 [5 juillet 1940]). Decades later, she still found it necessary, in an interview given to her biographer Deirdre Bair, to compare

her former lover to 'violent, destructive weather: beautiful to
look at if you were not subject to it, leaving horrible destruction
and desolation in its wake'(p. 237). The obliteration of Hélène
that takes place within the fictional boundaries of *Le Sang des
autres* may be related to the desiring difficulties, and the
resultant 'nervosité'(*LS II*, p. 160 [11 juillet 1940]), which the
above observations indicate to have been Beauvoir's wartime
lot. Biographically speaking, Hélène 'is' both Beauvoir and
Sorokine; is, in other words, at once a self-projection and a
projection of the (disturbing) Other / lover. She is, moreover,
particularly in the early chapters of *Le Sang des autres*,
(troubled) sensuality. By suppressing Hélène textually, what
Beauvoir is doing, arguably, is on some level to suppress not
only an element of her *own* sensuality which she found
increasingly difficult to contain, but also the female partner-in-
desire whose presence in her life turned out, after all, to be far
less easy to 'manage' than she had believed or expected. As the
narrative thread of *Le Sang des autres* unwinds, Hélène is
deprived of her life and, to a degree, of her voice. In taking
these away from her, Beauvoir—in the eyes, at least, of the
resolutely biographical critic—is effecting a controlling, self-
protective, textual gesture by means of which she can deflect,
conjure and negate both the appeal of female homo-eroticism
(incarnated, existentially, by Nathalie Sorokine) and her own
personal response to it. Tellingly, as Beauvoir tartly indicates
in her correspondence with Sartre, Sorokine herself found her
friend's fictional production unpalatable ('J'ai eu une lettre de
Sorokine qui vomit *Le Sang des autres* mais pour des raisons
très sottes, essentiellement parce que ça l'ennuie'—*LS II*, p. 251
[janvier 1944]).

As elements of this discussion have already implied, the
issue of desire—or, rather, of how we interpret it—is, to a
degree, bound up in *Le Sang des autres* with the issue of
control. In her analysis of gender and narrative in *L'Invitée*,
Martha Evans argues that the inclusion in Beauvoir's
autobiographical writings of abundant commentaries on her
fictional texts represents 'a pre-emptive move' on their
author's part: a move aimed at obliging her readers to make
particular, 'guided' analyses of her fictions (see p. 70). Evans's
comments—which foreground the key question of who controls
the Beauvoirian text—enable us to reflect productively upon

the dynamics of our readerly encounter with Beauvoir's second novel and, more particularly, with the love scenario it stages. If, as readers of *Le Sang des autres*, we do no more than endorse and adhere to the (existentialist, Hélène-oriented) interpretation of that scenario which is set up in *La Force de l'âge*, then arguably we become the playthings of Beauvoir's extratextual, authorial authority, a ('male') authority which, according to Evans's feminist analysis, Beauvoir's enduring ambivalence about her own gender drove her to protect and pursue. As we have seen, however, the reader of *Le Sang des autres* can read 'otherwise'; can evolve a non-sanctioned, 'readerly' exegesis of Beauvoir's text and its desiring dynamics which exceeds the parameters of Beauvoir's 'authorial interpretation'. S/he can, by taking this exegesis to its limits, go so far as to frame such a fictional production as a personal exercise in sexual control; as the site, even, of a (displaced, unacknowledged) foreclosure of her own, 'aberrant' feminine/ lesbian sexuality whose ultimate manifestation is the 'dépouille' of Hélène's sentient, sensual body (309).

What are the consequences of departing from the sanctioned exegetical path upon which Beauvoir's 'authorial interpretation' sets us? How does doing so situate us vis-à-vis Beauvoir herself? For Evans, the ineluctable existence of her pre-emptive, autobiographical self-readings 'turns the task of the critic, whose place has already been taken by the author, into an act of antagonism'(p. 70) Reading 'against', i.e. differently from, Beauvoir, eluding her authorial control, involves us, then, in a form of hostility, of 'betrayal' even. For certain readers, particularly feminists, indulging in critical antagonism of this kind cannot help but engender unease. However, once we, as critics, begin to address the complexities of Beauvoir's writings and to explore the maelstrom of emotions and compulsions which are obscured by her own rationalizing, 'peremptory' auto-interpretations, then readerly 'treachery' becomes an unavoidable—if regrettable— phenomenon.

Chapter Three

Narrative strategies

The preceding discussion has already touched in passing upon the issue of the narrative strategies Beauvoir deploys in her second novel; however, the formal and technical dimensions of her text merit further, closer scrutiny. We have noted already the oscillations of narrative voice and point of view present within *Le Sang des autres*. We have remarked too upon the way in which, on occasion, these oscillations inflect or inhibit our capacity entirely to elucidate certain aspects of Beauvoir's text (notably her heroine's intimate relation to desire and sexuality). The fragmentation of narrative perspective that characterizes *Le Sang des autres*—a fragmentation similarly in evidence in Sartre's 'war novels' *Le Sursis* (1945) and *La Mort dans l'âme* (1949)—may be read as symptomatic of an attempt on Beauvoir's part to convey kaleidoscopically rather than univocally the realities and ramifications of a particular and critical political and historical moment. It is a discursive feature present, Keefe informs us, in a number of other French existentialist texts in which collective situations and the effect upon them of the powerful forces of History constitute a key focus (1986, pp. 89-90).

Alternatively, Beauvoir's oscillatory manipulation of voice and viewpoint may be contextualised in terms of the intricacies of the love-story 'strand' of her novel. This is because the hierarchised narrative relation which that manipulation sets up between the (longer, privileged, 'absorbing') Blomart-focalised chapters and the (shorter, 'absorbed') Hélène-focused sections of the text may be taken to emblematize, on the level of *discours*, the power dynamics of the *histoire affective* offered to us by *Le Sang des autres*, one which, as we saw above, is predicated upon a (gendered) emotional disequilibrium and culminates—arguably—in Blomart's murderous 'erasure' of Hélène. But what of narrative structure and development in *Le Sang des autres*? Clearly, the events and details of Beauvoir's story are disposed in a highly complicated, at times confusing fashion. How might their organisation be explained?

Le Sang des autres is, if we adopt Roland Barthes's analysis of reading codes, a novel in which a dominant role is afforded to the hermeneutic stratum, i.e. to that 'ensemble des unités [narratives] qui ont pour fonction d'articuler, de diverse manières, une question, sa réponse et les accidents variés qui peuvent préparer ou retarder sa réponse'.[1] Beauvoir's text exemplifies what Seymour Chatman describes as 'the traditional narrative of resolution', in so far as it conveys, powerfully, 'a sense of problem-solving, of things being worked out in some way, of a kind of ratiocinative or emotional teleology'.[2] It begins (11) by signalling the existence of a dilemma, the precise, essentially moral nature of which (should Blomart sanction the act of sabotage which Laurent and the others seek to set in train, thereby putting human life at risk, or not?) is only gradually revealed to the reader. It terminates once Blomart succeeds—however provisionally and problematically—in solving that dilemma. It is in terms of Beauvoir's determinedly hermeneutic (and ethical) emphasis that the evolutionary narrative modalities of *Le Sang des autres*—specifically the existence within the text of a dual as opposed to a single chronology—can and must be understood.

The first of the novel's two chronological sequences is that of the narrative 'now', and its immediate prehistory. In evidence in the odd-numbered chapters of the text, and omnipresent in chapter XIII, this sequence charts Blomart's *veillée* at his lover's bedside and records the events of the night through which it lasts. It is punctuated by the painful reflections and hesitations that accompany the decision-making process upon which he is embarked, and reaches its climax, in tandem with Beauvoir's 'histoire', when Blomart finally gives Laurent his answer. It is a key source/site of the suspense with which, as she reveals in *La Force de l'âge*, Beauvoir sought to imbue her tale ('Pour éviter que ses ruminations fussent oiseuses, je créai un *suspense:* à l'aube, donnerait-il, ne donnerait-il pas le signal d'un nouvel attentat?'—*FA*, p. 626). The second (and major) temporal sequence of Beauvoir's narrative is that generated by its series of analeptic flashbacks, the presence of which infuses her tale

---

[1] Roland Barthes, *S/Z* (Paris: Seuil, 1970), p. 11.
[2] Seymour Chatman, *Story and Discourse: Narrative Structure in Fiction and Film* (Cornell University Press, 1978), p. 48.

with a melodramatic, classically 'cinematic' atmosphere. It incorporates the Hélène-focused chapters in their entirety and takes in, too, those central segments of the Blomart-oriented chapters in which his thoughts are impelled by 'present' events and reflections backwards towards the / his (more distant) past, and towards the crises, dilemmas and doubts of that past. 'Sequence 2' offers us, *inter alia*—notably in the odd-numbered chapters—chronologically-organised information which enables us to comprehend more completely *why* and *how* it is that Blomart can arrive eventually at the particular decision about / solution to the sabotage issue which he articulates in chapter XIII. It confirms Susan Hayward's argument that (cinematic) flashbacks are 'hermeneutically determined'; that, 'by nature investigative or confessional narrative codes', they 'almost always serve to resolve an enigma'.[3]

The treatment of time in *Le Sang des autres* is extremely complex, as Beauvoir herself admits:

> Je respectais l'ordre chronologique; mais, par moments, l'actualité brisait l'évocation des jours anciens. J'y emmêlai aussi, en les soulignant par des italiques, les pensées, les émotions qu'éprouvait Blomart au cours de la nuit. [...] Toutes les dimensions du temps se trouvaient rassemblées dans cette veillée funèbre: le héros le vivait au présent, en s'interrogeant à travers son passé sur une décision qui engageait son avenir. Cette construction convenait au sujet. (*FA*, p. 626)

This is particularly apparent in the Blomart, odd-numbered chapters, in which, rather than constituting wholly discrete entities, the dual temporal sequences of the text insistently inflect and tangle with each other. The key point about both of these chronological, structuring strands is, however, that they work in tandem in order to guide the reader ineluctably toward Blomart's eventual 'je suis d'accord', furnishing at the same time an understanding of the rationale behind, and the ethical stance embodied in, his concluding remark. Together, they generate and compel us along a readerly 'track' leading forcefully towards that ultimate moment of moral, metaphysical resolution / choice with which—to the reader's

---

[3] Susan Hayward, *Key Concepts in Cinema* (London and New York: Routledge, forthcoming).

relief and satisfaction—*Le Sang des autres* culminates. The effect of this is to make Beauvoir's novel into a text with an extremely—and apparently exclusively—linear, goal-oriented narrative structure. This structure, evidently, is a function of the hermeneutic, 'teleological' (to borrow Chatman's term) nature of Beauvoir's chronicle of dilemmas and decisions.

Once the above details have been recorded, it might seem that little remains to be said about the structural organisation of *Le Sang des autres*. However, a careful investigation of Beauvoir's text reveals it in fact to contain an alternative or secondary structural paradigm. This is generated by that body of recurring motifs and themes which, scattered throughout *Le Sang des autres*, cannot help, by virtue of their proliferation, but impinge upon the consciousness of the reader. There is insufficient space here to trace the textual manifestations of each and every one of the novel's recurring rhetorical figures. We will focus, therefore, on just three of them. These are:

i) the motif of bloodiness

This motif—evocative, evidently, of mortality and death—is emphasized by repeated references to 'sang' itself on pages 17; 19; 22; 70; 75; 89; 95; 105; 125; 129; 131; 134; 137; 149; 150; 151; 154; 156; 161; 169; 176; 222; 224; 233; 238; 244; 245; 257; 274; 282; 289. With reference to things / entities (including human skin) that are 'roses', 'rouges' or 'rougis', on pages 25; 29; 44; 50; 59; 84; 90; 99; 113; 117; 125; 130; 142; 156; 165; 183; 184; 187-91; 215; 220; 230; 237-8; 269; 277; 282; 296; 301; 306. And with reference to the red / white colour combination already cited in Chapter Two of this study in connection with Blomart's unconscious, 'matricidal' impulses vis-à-vis his mistress—pages 16; 19; 21; 38; 42; 71; 86; 125; 129; 131; 132; 150; 160-61; 220; 256; 257; 264; 272; 274; 287; 291. Curiously, in chapter VII (numerically, the fulcrum of *Le Sang des autres*), the redness / blood motif—present in some form in each of the other twelve sections of the text—disappears completely.

ii) the motif of mother/child division

Signals illuminating this motif, many of which involve a reference to a potential or actual death, are to be found on pages 15; 16-18; 19; 45; 123; 230; 232; 238; 259-61; 281; 289; 293; 294; 295; 296; 305. Mother / child couples who risk or undergo some form of detachment or loss in *Le Sang des autres* are: Louise and her dead baby; Blomart and Madame Blomart; Yvonne and the hypochondriac Mme Kotz; Ruth and her mother, whose arrest and separation Hélène witnesses in chapter XII; the woman and child pair who make their appearance in chapter X. Fallaize and Atack independently note the key structural function accorded to the mother / child motif in Beauvoir's text.

iii) the motif of food-as-problem

Le Sang des autres repeatedly evokes the process of ingestion. References pinpointing, specifically, the discomfiture- or anxiety-inducing character of food and eating—references which frequently highlight the theme of social or moral culpability—are to be found on pages 16-18; 24; 27; 36; 38; 41; 72; 114; 151; 156; 184; 186; 200-201; 230; 236; 240; 241; 256; 260; 262-3; 269; 272; 275; 289; 294.

The theme or image 'clusters' whose existence is indicated by the above, somewhat laborious cataloguing of Beauvoir's novel belong to the 'obsessional' aspect of *Le Sang des autres*. It is certainly possible in some way to relate each of them (most obviously the first and the third) to the ethical debate which Beauvoir's text stages, and to the question of man's 'fatal' impingement upon, and responsibility to, the Other which lies at the heart of that debate. However, these 'clusters' are clearly not wholly or exclusively connected to the moral issues which *Le Sang des autres* raises. They constitute, rather, pointers to what might be termed the novel's Unconscious. They attest to its most intimate proccupations and fantasms. They are evocative, arguably, of issues of a psychological, primordial nature: issues such as the initiatory trauma of mother / child symbiosis and separation, the invasive nature of the eating / feeding process, the terror that inheres to the (necessary) demise of the (m)other and the more general horror intrinsic in human mortality. These are issues which are insistently present elsewhere in Beauvoir's writing, which are a highly personal feature of her work, and which have been dissected at length by a number of Beauvoirian critics (see for example Marks; Evans [1986]; Jardine; Hughes; Moi [1994]).

In structural terms, the effect of the presence, within *Le Sang des autres*, of these repetition-based 'clusters' is to create a sense of narrative circularity, of stasis even. The subterranean, aesthetic / obsessional, immobilizing structural pattern they generate offsets or undermines that linear, chronological construction whose relationship to Beauvoir's resolutionary narrative project and ethical aim we have already established. *Le Sang des autres* constitutes, in other words, a text that seems ultimately to be inwardly at odds with itself, and with its hermeneutic, goal-oriented intent. What are we to make of this curious, conflictual narrative phenomenon? We may choose simply to view it as symptomatic somehow of that unease inspired in Beauvoir in the early 1940s by the (excessively?) ethico-didactic character of her novel, and by the constraints intrinsic to the writerly phase in which she was caught up. Can we, however, gain alternative purchases on it?

In her analysis of Beauvoir's autobiographical writings (which date from 1958), Jane Heath remarks upon 'the smooth consistency of Beauvoir's autobiographies, the conscious organisation of the discourse according to a project'(p. 9), and isolates these narrative features as determining characteristics of Beauvoir's exercises in self-representation.[4] Heath notes, further, the tension that exists between the textual, teleological, 'repressive' cohesiveness Beauvoir patently strove to foreground in her personal writings (and elsewhere), and 'the stress points where it seems threatened, most likely to collapse' (*ibid.*). For Heath, this tension is exemplified in Beauvoir's autobiographies by the 'fascinating interaction between two narrative modes: a linear, chronological (and chronic) mode which figures the 'I' of the *énoncé*, of the statement, and a discourse which figures the 'I' of the *énonciation*, which retrospectively shapes and organises the linear narrative (the main narrative) and whose effect is to undercut its authority'(p. 58). It derives, she suggests, from the fact that whilst Beauvoir's intellectual, 'male-identified' writerly persona succumbed consistently to the lure of that

---

[4] Heath cites Margaret Walters's 1976 essay 'The Rights and Wrongs of Women' as the source of her observations here.

'drive towards coherence'(p. 54) which emblematizes rational, ordered, 'masculine' discourse, she was enduringly haunted by a troubling 'return of the feminine'(p. 9). The discursive manifestations of this return, Heath argues, are evidenced by those narrative elements within Beauvoir's autobiographies which are marginal to, and which undermine, the cohesion and order of her main / 'male', teleo-chronological narrative mode.

Heath is exploiting here the post-structuralist, psychoanalytic argument that men's and women's different, unconscious relations to the Phallus give rise to different relations to language and to different modes of discourse— modes which, we should note, *both* sexes may employ (see Heath, 'Introduction'). Her gender-related reading of Beauvoir's autobiographical narrative strategies—a reading which foregrounds the notion that her subject 'spoke predominantly the discourse of repression, allowed the man in her to speak' (p. 9)—is typical of a broader body of radical feminist textual criticism. It is not without its problems, not least amongst which is the over-simplistic sexualisation of discursive models upon which it relies. However, it is useful to us in so far as it enables us to view the narrative paradigm governing *Le Sang des autres*—based as it is on an unsettled, unsettling pull between goal-oriented cohesion and repetitive, disruptive circularity—as somehow characteristic of Beauvoirian writing in general. Heath's remarks permit us, in other words, to contextualize the narrative workings of Beauvoir's second novel in terms of discursive 'conflicts' that prove in fact to be enduringly present within her *oeuvre*, rather than in terms of the particular discontents engendered by the 'période morale' of her literary trajectory. We are not obliged, in 'Heathian' vein, to read the conflictual narrative / structural modalities contained in *Le Sang des autres* as evidence of Beauvoir's ambivalent and problematic relation to discursive gender-identification—although we may find it tempting and productive so to do. However, we can and should regard these modalities as symptomatic of a broader, ongoing tendency on Beauvoir's part to produce teleological, chronological, would-be consistent narratives which somehow 'betray' themselves from within, thereby revealing a deep-seated ambivalence on the part of their creator towards the (ultra-controlled) narrative form in which authority has been vested.

Conclusion

Le Sang des autres is hardly Beauvoir's most popular novel; indeed, it may be classed amongst her least widely-read—and least frequently taught—works of fiction. We need to ask ourselves why this might be the case. First, we must remember that *Le Sang des autres* is a very early Beauvoirian creation. The juvenilia of most authors—unless they succeed, as *L'Invitée* has done, in belatedly capturing the critical imagination—tend to be disregarded in favour of their more mature and polished works, which stand a far higher chance of acceding to 'canonical' status. Then there is the (related) fact of the narrative complexity of Beauvoir's novel. The convoluted character of the narrative 'tricks' present within *Le Sang des autres*, especially chapter I, suggests that Beauvoir had not yet fully mastered the technical virtuosity of which she was evidently in pursuit (she achieved it in her later fictions), and may prove rebarbative for some readers.

A rapid perusal of the entry devoted to *Le Sang des autres* by Joy Bennett and Gabriella Hochman, in their extremely useful *Simone de Beauvoir: an Annotated Bibliography*, provides us with further insight into the marginalisation to which this novel has fallen victim. They list—by no means exhaustively—reviews which appeared in France, the United States and Britain upon the publication of *Le Sang des autres* and its English translation (sadly, Gallimard's *dossier de presse* on the text has been destroyed). The authors of the majority of these, even when electing to praise Beauvoir's novel (as many did), express their conviction that it represents first and foremost a fictional exegesis of issues raised by existentialist moral thought. For hostile critics—incensed by the 'dull, disjointed, intellectualized affair'[1] created by Beauvoir, and by the 'unconvincing mouthpieces' of existentialist ethics who people its pages[2]—this factor was precisely the source of the literary defects they imputed to *Le Sang des autres*.

---

[1] J.R. Newman, 'The Lady Doth Protest', *New Republic*, 2 August 1948, pp. 24-6.

[2] J. Stern, 'Imported from France', *New York Times*, 25 July 1948, p. 14.

As like as not, critics of this latter type were motivated by
personal preconceptions and prejudices. In the late 1940s and
1950s, Beauvoir, Sartre and their writings were subject to
considerable opprobrium within and outside France. An
observation contained in a letter Beauvoir sent Sartre during
her first trip to America is not unilluminating in this context:

> J'ai trouvé dans l'appartement [de la dame des relations
> culturelles] un vieux professeur français de Harvard,
> immonde, qui m'a fait la cuisine et des grâces et dont j'ai su
> par la suite qu'il était un de ceux qui voulaient m'empêcher
> de venir, par haine de l'existentialisme. (*LS II*, 30 janvier
> 1947, p. 282)

However, the existence of antagonistic critical judgements of
the kind cited above—pre-programmed and biased as they may
well have been—attests to the fact that *Le Sang des autres*, qua
intellectual / philosophical discussion, possesses the potential to
alienate and irritate the reader, for all the sophistication and
complexity of its ethical, metaphysical plot-line. This
phenomenon undoubtedly helps to explain why Beauvoir's
novel does not occupy a more privileged position within her
pantheon of fiction.

In the light of the above, should we conclude that *Le Sang
des autres* is an 'inferior' Beauvoirian text, a text that is
somehow less deserving of continued critical attention than
other elements of her *oeuvre*? Indeed not. For one thing, as we
have already established, Beauvoir's second novel offers an
intricate—and troubling—dissection of the dynamics of human
involvement. Its tableau of desire, denial and death patently
constitutes more than just an arid ethical dissertation produced
by a high-minded blue-stocking capable only of writing 'moody
philosophical tracts'.[3] The insights and silences which inhere in
that tableau cannot help but fascinate contemporary critical
readers keen to explore processes of sex- and gender-
representation, and to reflect in so doing on the complexities of
Beauvoir's own, gendered relationship to writing. Secondly,
the 'documentary', historico-political dimension of *Le Sang des
autres* makes Beauvoir's fictional creation an obvious target
for those readers and scholars drawn to address the issue and

---

[3] G. Herzog, 'Feeling Gloomy? Try this...', *Chicago Sun*, 21 July 1948, p. 57.

the function of literature as social *témoignage*. Furthermore, as elements of this discussion have intimated, Beauvoir's novel —containing as it does evidence of themes, preoccupations and discursive tropes which prove to be hallmarks of her *œuvre*— displays an intertextual dimension on which critical work undoubtedly remains to be done, and which adds significantly to its interpretative 'capital'. Finally, we must not forget that Beauvoirian criticism is currently undergoing something of a sea-change, provoked by the belated publication of Beauvoir's most intimate writings and by the debates these writings have engendered. *Le Sang des autres* is a text which will indubitably benefit from a detailed, biographically-oriented reappraisal, some of the preliminaries of which have been sketched out (pp. 46-51) in the middle section of this study.

Glossary
of existentialist terminology

Being-for-others / *être-pour-autrui*

An ontological category deriving from the fact that we exist as objects for and in other consciousnesses. This phenomenon is liable to inspire disquiet and engender conflict. Cranston glosses Sartre's account of being-for-others as follows: '[Others] see me as part of the furniture of their external world. They observe my behaviour. I, seeing them see me, [...] acquire, through them, this added form of being which Sartre calls being "for-others". [...] In so far as the look of another person turns me into an object, it turns me into something "solidified", something with a character; and so, in a sense, it takes away my freedom' (Cranston, pp. 53-4).

Consciousness

Otherwise known as the *pour-soi* / 'for-itself'. Consciousness is consciousness of something; it cannot exist without objects. It is what perceives—and is differentiated from—objects, things, the immutability and chaos of the world (the *en-soi* / 'in-itself'). Unlike the in-itself, consciousness, while it has a tendency towards inertia, is moreover able to change, evolve and to question itself. It 'moves all the time, and it sees itself as a nihilation of its own past being'(*ibid.*, p. 47). Consciousness— the characteristic experience of which is choice / metamorphosis—is what allows human beings to recreate and transcend themselves perpetually.

Contingency / *contingence*

This signifies the 'brute fact of being' (Leak, p. 154). The hero of Sartre's novel *La Nausée* (1938), Antoine Roquentin, discovers contingency when he realises that everything and every being that exists, including himself, is devoid of inherent necessity and justification; that existence is gratuitous. Contingency is the point of departure for Sartre's examination of human reality.

Facticity / *facticité*

Facticity subsumes all of those things / factors which form part of our situation without, however, having been chosen by us, and which in consequence seem devoid of rational justification. As Leak puts it, 'my body, my past, my birth (in a certain place, at a certain time, into a certain class etc) are all aspects of facticity, inasmuch as they were not chosen' (p. 155).

Immanence / *immanence*

A key term in *Le Deuxième Sexe*. Moi states that 'most precisely defined as non-transcendence, immanence [...] would seem to include everything from the state of thing-like facticity sought by the for-itself to bad faith and various kinds of unfree situations' (Moi, 1994, p. 154).

Transcendence / *transcendance*

This notion signifies that potential for ongoing, willed self-(re)construction and self-redefinition, via freely chosen projects, which for Sartre is what marks us out as human. It suggests a kind of forward movement into the future. According to Beauvoir, 'la transcendance est un perpétuel dépassement' (*PC*, p. 35). For Leak, transcendence is 'consciousness itself as it goes past the given towards its own possibilities' (p. 158).

Select Bibliography

Where not otherwise indicated, place of publication for books written in English is London, and written in French, Paris.

Texts cited in this study are designated by the given acronyms.

1. Beauvoir's Major Works

L'Invitée. Gallimard, 1943.

Pyrrhus et Cinéas. NRF Gallimard , 1944 (*PC*).

Le Sang des autres. Gallimard (Folio), 1945.

Les Bouches inutiles. Gallimard, 1945.

Tous les hommes sont mortels. Gallimard, 1945.

Pour une morale de l'ambiguïté, Gallimard, 'Idées', 1947 (*PMA*).

L'Amérique au jour le jour. Morihien, 1948.

Le Deuxième Sexe. Gallimard (Folio, 2 volumes), 1949 (*DS*).

Les Mandarins, Gallimard, 1954.

Mémoires d'une jeune fille rangée, Folio (Gallimard), 1958.

La Force de l'âge, Livre de Poche (NRF Gallimard), 1960 (*FA*).

La Force des choses, Gallimard, 1963.

Une mort très douce. Gallimard, 1964.

Les Belles Images, Gallimard, 1966.

La Femme rompue, Gallimard, 1968.

La Vieillesse, Gallimard, 1970.

Tout compte fait, Gallimard, 1972.

Quand prime le spirituel, Gallimard, 1979.

La Cérémonie des adieux, Gallimard, 1981.

Journal de guerre, NRF Gallimard, 1990 (*JG*).

Lettres à Sartre, NRF Gallimard, (2 volumes), 1990 (*LS*).

2. Critical Works on Beauvoir and *Le Sang des autres*

Ascher, Carol, *Simone de Beauvoir: A Life of Freedom*. Brighton: Harvester, 1981.

Bair, Deirdre, *Simone de Beauvoir: A Biography*. Jonathan Cape, 1990.

Blanchot, Maurice, *La Part du feu* (Gallimard, 1949), pp. 195-211.

Crosland, Margaret, *Simone de Beauvoir: The Woman and her Work*. Heinemann, 1992.

d'Eaubonne, Françoise, *Une femme nommée Castor, mon amie*. Encre, 1986.

Evans, Martha Noel, 'Murdering *L'Invitée*: Gender and Fictional Narrative', in Wenzel, Hélène (ed.), *Yale French Studies*, 72 (1986), 67-86.

Evans, Mary, *Simone de Beauvoir: A Feminist Mandarin*. Tavistock, 1985.

Fallaize, Elizabeth, *The Novels of Simone de Beauvoir*. Routledge, 1988.

Francis, Claude, and Gonthier, Fernande, *Les Écrits de Simone de Beauvoir*. Gallimard, 1979.

Fullbrook, Kate and Fullbrook, Edward, *Simone de Beauvoir and Jean-Paul Sartre: The Remaking of a Twentieth-Century Legend*. Hemel Hempstead: Harvester Wheatsheaf, 1993.

Gennari, Geneviève, *Simone de Beauvoir*. Éditions Universitaires, 1958.

Heath, Jane, *Simone de Beauvoir*. Brighton: Harvester, 1989.

Hughes, Alex 'Murdering the Mother: Simone de Beauvoir's *Mémoires d'une jeune fille rangée'*, *French Studies*, XLVII, 2 (April 1994), 175-83.

Jardine, Alice, 'Death Sentences: Writing Couples and Ideology', in Marks, Elaine (ed.), *Critical Essays on Simone de Beauvoir*. Boston: Hall, 1987, pp.207-218.

Keefe, Terry, *Simone de Beauvoir: A Study of her Writings*. Harrap, 1983.

——————, *Beauvoir:'Les Belles Images'/'La Femme rompue*. UNIVERSITY OF GLASGOW FRENCH & GERMAN PUBLICATIONS, 1991.

Leighton, Jean, *Simone de Beauvoir on Women*. Cranbury, N.J.: Associated University Presses, 1975.

Low, Peter, 'Simone de Beauvoir's Wartime Novel *Le Sang des autres* et les yeux de l'auteur', *New Zealand Journal of French Studies*, 13 (1992), 25-36.

Marks, Elaine, *Simone de Beauvoir: Encounters with Death*. New Brunswick, N.J.: Rutgers University Press, 1973.

Moi, Toril, *Feminist Theory and Simone de Beauvoir*. Oxford: Blackwell, 1990.

——————, *Simone de Beauvoir: The Making of an Intellectual Woman*. Cambridge, Mass. and Oxford: Blackwell, 1994.

Okely, Judith, *Simone de Beauvoir*. Virago, 1986.

Ophir, Anne, *Regards féminins: Beauvoir/ Etcherelli/ Rochefort*. Denoël, 1976.

Patterson, Yolanda, *Simone de Beauvoir and the Demystification of Motherhood*. Ann Arbor and London: UNI Research Press, 1989.

——————, 'Simone de Beauvoir and the Demystification of Motherhood' in Wenzel, Hélène (ed.), *Yale French Studies*, 72 (1986), 87-105.

Rochester, Myrna Bell and Lawrence, Mary, 'Simone de Beauvoir: Living through Conflict', *Journal of Simone de Beauvoir Studies*, 9 (1992), 17-30.

Simons, Margaret, 'Beauvoir and Sartre: The Philosophical Relationship' in Wenzel, Hélène (ed.), *Yale French Studies*, 72 (1986), 165-79.

Singer, Linda, 'Interpretation and Revival: Rereading Beauvoir', *Women's Studies International Forum*, 8 (1985), 231-8.

Walters, Margaret, 'The Rights and Wrongs of Women: Mary Wollstonecraft, Harriet Martineau and Simone de Beauvoir', in Oakley, Anne and Mitchell, Juliet (eds.), *The Rights and Wrongs of Women*. Harmondsworth: Penguin, 1976, pp. 304-78.

Whitmarsh, Anne, *Simone de Beauvoir and the Limits of Commitment*. Cambridge University Press, 1981.

Wilson, Emma, 'Daughters and Desire: Simone de Beauvoir's *Journal de guerre*', in Keefe, Terry and Smyth, Edmund (eds.), *Autobiography and the Existential Self: Studies in Modern French Writing* (Liverpool University Press, 1994), pp. 83-98.

Winegarten, Renée, *Simone de Beauvoir: A Critical View*. Oxford: Berg, 1988.

3. Background and Further Reading

Atack, Margaret, *Literature and the French Resistance*. Manchester University Press, 1989.

Barthes, Roland, *S/Z*. Seuil, 1970.

Chatman, Seymour, *Story and Discourse: Narrative Structure in Fiction and Film*. Ithaca and London: Cornell University Press, 1978.

Cranston, Maurice, *Sartre*. Edinburgh: Oliver and Boyd, 'Writers and Critics', 1962.

Freud, Sigmund: see the volumes in the *Pelican Freud Library* (Harmondsworth: Penguin, 1973–) on 'Sexuality' (vol 7), 'Case Histories' (vols. 8-9) and 'The Interpretation of Dreams' (vol. 14).

Harris, Frederick, *Encounters with Darkness: French and German Writers on World War II*. New York and Oxford: Oxford University Press, 1983.

Higgins, Ian (ed.), *The Second World War in Literature*. Scottish Academic Press, 1986.

Howells, Christina, *The Cambridge Companion to Sartre*. Cambridge University Press, 1992.

Kedward, H.R., *Occupied France: Collaboration and Resistance*. Oxford: Blackwell, 1985.

Keefe, Terry, *French Existentialist Fiction: Changing Moral Perspectives*. Beckenham: Croom Helm, 1986.

Leak, Andrew, *The Perverted Consciousness: Sexuality and Sartre*. Macmillan, 1989.

Michel, Henri, *Histoire de la résistance*. PUF, 'Que sais-je?', 1972.

Ory, Pascal and Sirinelli, Jean-François, *Les Intellectuels en France, de l'Affaire Dreyfus à nos jours*. A. Colin, 1986.

Péan, Pierre, *Une jeunesse française: François Mitterrand 1934-1947*. Fayard, 1994.

Prost, Antoine, *Petite Histoire de la France au XXe siècle*. A. Colin, 1979.

Sartre, Jean-Paul, *L'Être et le néant*. Gallimard, 1943 (*EN*).

——————————, *L'Existentialisme est un humanisme*. Nagel, 1946.

——————————, *Situations II*. Gallimard, 1948.

Segal, Naomi, *Narcissus and Echo: Women in the French 'récit'*. Manchester University Press, 1988.

Suleiman, Susan, *Authoritarian Fictions: the Ideological Novel as a Literary Genre*. Princeton University Press, 1983.

Wright, Elizabeth, *Psychoanalytic Criticism: Theory in Practice*. New York and London: Methuen, 1984.